CW01369242

The Follies of
BOUGHTON PARK

*"The park and adjacent grounds,
which are partly walled, were well wooded;
and temples, triumphal arches,
and artificial ruins, were interspersed
in fantastic variety."*

George Baker
*The History and Antiquities of the
County of Northamptonshire*
1822

SCOTT PUBLICATIONS
1995

*To my parents – for their love,
understanding and encouragement.*

By the same author:
Formula One Drivers' Profiles, 1982.

First published in 1995 by:
SCOTT PUBLICATIONS
Moulton, Northampton NN3 7SH
Telephone: 01604 642411

Copyright © Simon Scott 1995

All rights reserved. No part of this book may be reproduced or transmitted in any form or by any means, electronic or mechanical, including photocopying, recording or by any information storage or retrieval system, without the written permission of the publisher.

British Library Cataloguing in Publication Data.
A catalogue record for this book is available from the British Library.

ISBN 0 9525366 5 X

Design and Artwork: Rowan Designs, Northampton.
Print: Impress Printers, Corby.

Contents

Foreword	4
Acknowledgements	5
Introduction	7
The Earls of Strafford	9
Horace Walpole and other influences	18
Boughton Hall	25
Boughton Park	30
The Hawking Tower	41
The Grotto	44
The Obelisk	46
The Spectacle	50
New Park Barn	53
Bunkers Hill Farm	55
Other landscape structures	59
The Church of St John the Baptist	62
Holly Lodge	66
The problem today	68
Notes	70

Foreword

The national love of gardening in its widest sense is by no means new, as is reflected by England's great wealth of historic gardens and parks. It perhaps comes as a surprise, then, to find how patchy our knowledge is of the development of many of our finest designed landscapes. There frequently is no readily available answer to questions such as who designed them and for what purpose? Who altered them and why? What fashions, aesthetics, or financial circumstances drove the changes? How did they evolve to reach their present form?

In view of this interest, it is puzzling, too, how a landscape with a pedigree of the length and quality of Boughton Park could slide into relative obscurity. That the estate is now in divided ownership, and so has ceased to be seen or considered as a single concept, may offer at least a partial explanation.

Simon Scott first contacted me early in February 1994, to express concern that one of the options for the proposed Northampton north-west bypass was shown as cutting right through the heart of Boughton Park. He was sure it was a park of quality which deserved protection.

Simon kindly showed me round the site and it was clear that it was indeed a landscape worthy of note. Information on the history of the landscape, however, was fragmentary, and it was difficult to judge its true importance.

Determined to fill in the gaps in our understanding of the history of the site, Simon's subsequent detailed research has amply supported his initial feelings. His findings have confirmed the site as being of such historic interest as fully to merit inclusion in the national *Register of Parks and Gardens* compiled by English Heritage.

With the publication of this book, rich in detail and generously illustrated, the fascinating history of the development of the park at Boughton into a fine eighteenth-century landscape, embellished with intriguing Gothic follies, can now be enjoyed by a wide audience.

Through Simon's energy and commitment, Boughton Park's story, with, at its centre, Thomas and William Wentworth, Earls of Strafford, has been skilfully pieced together. No longer does the park languish unremembered; it has been brought again into focus as a landscape of national importance. There is now no excuse for not giving its historic interest full consideration in any decisions affecting its future.

Dr Harriet Jordan
Inspector of Historic Parks and Gardens, English Heritage
April 1995

Acknowledgements

Researching the history of an eighteenth-century landscape park, I now know, can be like searching for the proverbial needle in a haystack. There are so many false leads, so many strands of information to bring together. There are also so many people who have given their help and advice without whom this book (much expanded from my article in *Follies* magazine) would never have become a reality.

Special thanks to: Dr Harriet Jordan, Inspector of Historic Parks and Gardens at English Heritage, who so readily agreed to write the foreword for this book – she was also the first to visit me and tour Boughton Park and it was her infectious enthusiasm that first prompted me to find out more about the park; Andrew Plumridge and Michael Cousins, respectively Secretary and Membership Secretary of the Folly Fellowship, who have been very supportive, Andrew with his campaigning letter-writing and Michael with his patience in answering my many obscure questions and who so kindly volunteered for the onerous task of checking this work; and David Lambert, Conservation Officer of the Garden History Society, for his tremendous interest and regular supply of information. Also, to James Hasler and Martin Croft for so diligently reading this book in manuscript.

In addition I am grateful to the following individuals and organisations for their invaluable assistance: the staff who have assisted me during my research visits to the British Library and Manuscript Rooms, Northampton Record Office, Northampton Library Local History Section, Leicester University Library, Sheffield Archives, Sheffield Library Local History Section, the Devonshire Manuscript Collection at Chatsworth, the Royal Commission on Historic Manuscripts, the Bodleian Library in Oxford, St Mary's College Library in Twickenham and the Public Record Office at Kew; individuals from local, national and international organisations who have provided welcome assistance, including Francis Golding and David Jacques of the International Council on Monuments and Sites, Harriet Hawkes of the Georgian Group, Julie Fennelly of the Gothic Society, Francis Neale and Suzannah Fleming of the Temple Trust, Messrs Cashmore, Franklin and Samways of the Twickenham Local History Society, Stefan Boberek of the Northern College at Wentworth Castle, James Collett-White at Bedfordshire County Record Office, Nicholas Rogers of Sidney Sussex College in Cambridge, Mrs Sam Davies of the Bank of England, Joan Sussler of the Lewis Walpole Library in Connecticut, Moira Birks of the National Monuments Record, Nina Drummond of Bonhams and Dave Martin for access to his postcard collection; experts including Christopher Taylor, Christopher Thacker, Jeanette Ray, William Hawkes and Patrick Eyres; local historians Bruce Bailey, Susan Ranson, Bob Eady and David Seccull; knowledgeable local residents Anthony Jeyes, John Mackaness, Esmond Kimbell, Mary Rowden, Ron Hodnett and Keith Adams; journalists Julia Stewart and Trevor Cooper of the *Chronicle & Echo* for their continued publicity; Keith Clulow for his unstinting photographic assistance; and the present Earls of both Strafford and Bathurst who have shown such an interest in their forebears.

The photographs in the book are from my own collection, except where indicated. I gratefully acknowledge the individuals and organisations who have kindly allowed me to reproduce their photographs and maps which add so much to this volume.

I apologise if I have omitted anyone from this list, which I have tried to make as comprehensive as possible.

Introduction

For as long as I can remember, my first waking view has been the Spectacle — a fine Gothic castellated archway a mere hundred yards from my bedroom window. To me it is a familiar friend, a part of my family. When the sun shines its stone features look somehow serene and content. When it rains or snows it seems brooding and ominous.

Unfortunately, as is so often the case in life, it is only when the things that you hold dear are threatened that you feel so fortunate to have enjoyed their presence over the years. It fills you with a strong urge to do all that is humanly possible to protect and save the object of your affection. News of an impending bypass through the tranquil Boughton Park and its picturesque folly landscape was the spur for me to find out more of the history of this unique historic landscape and to campaign for its preservation.

As Marketing Services Manager at Haddonstone, well known for their classical garden ornaments and architectural stonework, I am in the unique position of owning a folly and publishing a book about follies, whilst also being involved with my Director, Alan Lorentzen, in the design of follies for the company's renowned exhibits at the Chelsea Flower Show.

There was a revival of the Gothic style of architecture in the first half of the eighteenth century. The earliest distinct types of building to incorporate the Gothic Revival style were ornamental landscape structures. Although nationally many of these landscape structures have since disappeared, we are lucky that at Boughton the structures have survived to enhance a landscape largely unchanged for more than 200 years.

The follies of Boughton Park are the largest collection of such structures in Northamptonshire and are now recognised as being of national importance. However, until now, their history has never been properly chronicled.

For the sake of historical accuracy, where possible I have quoted from original manuscripts. The reader should remember, however, that in the eighteenth century many words were either spelt phonetically or in a style not recognised today. For example, we find "horschessnutts" for horse chestnuts and "finnist" for finished. Any errors of fact or interpretation must, obviously, remain the responsibility of the author.

Simon Scott
Moulton
June 1995

The Earls of STRAFFORD

The Earls of Strafford,[1] in particular William Wentworth, the second Earl of the second creation (1722–91), are inexorably linked to the history of Boughton Park and the follies it contains.

The first Earl of Strafford, Thomas Wentworth (1593–1641), was a Yorkshire squire who rose to become Charles I's most able minister. Ireland, so often the graveyard of political reputations, was the path by which he chose to rise to power. By his determined policy he created an absolute government in Ireland and gained a favourable position for himself at Court with an impressive seat at Wentworth Woodhouse in Yorkshire. Ultimately, "the Great Strafford" was sacrificed by the King to an angry parliament on the eve of the Civil War, being executed on Tower Hill in 1641. His life and personality haunted the imagination of his family for generations, whilst his quotation on receipt of his death warrant, "Put not thy trust in princes", has passed into the proverbs of the English language.

The first Earl of the second creation was, in fact, the grand-nephew of the original first Earl. Also named Thomas Wentworth, he lived from 1672 to 1739. Deprived of the vast wealth and estates in England and Ireland that he considered to be his birthright – including the family seat of Wentworth Woodhouse – Thomas Wentworth derived the Barony of Raby only following the death of his cousin William, the second Earl of Strafford of the first creation.

Although bereft of money and land, as Baron of Raby, Thomas Wentworth had a seat in the House of Lords and a burning desire to achieve favour and influence. Although owning only a modest landholding, he rose quickly and steadily to become Colonel of the Royal Regiment of Dragoons and a friend and comrade-in-arms of William III. By 1703 Queen Anne had appointed him Envoy-Extraordinary to the Prussian Court in Berlin; becoming Ambassador-Extraordinary in 1706. In 1708 he purchased Stainborough Hall, later renamed Wentworth Castle, where he expanded the house and decorated the landscape with Gothic structures. Being adjacent to Wentworth Woodhouse, this purchase allowed him to return to the land of his illustrious ancestor.

By now, his career was seemingly spiralling ever upwards, Thomas Wentworth being appointed Ambassador-Extraordinary to the Dutch States General in The Hague, a Privy Councillor and Earl of Strafford of the second creation by the Tory government in 1711. This last honour was particularly cherished by Thomas Wentworth as it established him as the true successor to "the Great Strafford". In 1712 he became First Lord of the Admiralty and a Knight of the Garter. The following year he was a joint negotiator of the Treaty of Utrecht – a Tory-managed peace agreement that ended ten years of war with France.

His world crashed around him, however, following the death of Queen Anne in 1714. With the accession of George I, Whig influence led to the Tory Thomas Wentworth being recalled from The Hague and imprisoned in the Tower of London whilst impeachment proceedings were set in motion. Thomas Wentworth defended himself so effectively that these proceedings lost momentum and he was finally released in 1717, his career in public office over. By then, however, Thomas Wentworth had made enough money, aided by a judicious marriage to Anne Johnson, (the only daughter and heiress of a prosperous shipbuilder),[2] to be a considerable landowner with houses at St James's Square in London, Twickenham[3] in Middlesex and Stainborough[4] in Yorkshire with land in Frestone, Suffolk and Toddington, Bedfordshire.

It was against this backdrop that Thomas Wentworth purchased the Boughton and Pitsford estates in 1717.

First deprived of his birthright, now exiled from public office, Thomas Wentworth maintained a loathing for his usurpers at Wentworth Woodhouse whilst becoming a prominent Jacobite conspirator. Indeed, for his services to

Thomas Wentworth, first Earl Strafford of the second creation (1672–1739), who purchased the Boughton and Pitsford estates in 1717.
(Courtesy: Northern College)

the Jacobite cause, he was created unofficial Duke of Strafford in 1721 and Commander-in-Chief of His Majesty's forces north of the Humber by the titular King James III. Thomas Wentworth's Jacobite sentiments are perhaps not surprising when one realises that his mother, Isabella, was a Lady of the Bedchamber to Mary of Modena, Queen of James II at the time of the birth of the disputed Prince of Wales, afterwards known as the Pretender.

Thomas Wentworth took his bitter sense of injustice at being removed from public office to his grave, for in a codicil to his will, dated October 1739, he asked to be interred in a "coffin with my coat of arms deeply engraved upon it or embossed and under it the Titles I bore at the death of Queen Anne, that I was impeached the first parliament of King George the first for serving that great and good queen and the nation in the peace at Utrecht."[5]

The landscape structures he created at Wentworth Castle were often thinly disguised statements – each marking a political event, idea or alliance. He incorporated features into his garden at Wentworth Castle such as a mock castle, cascade and temple in a formal geometric layout, the style of which he would repeat at Boughton. Dating from 1726–30, perhaps Thomas Wentworth's most significant contribution to Gothic or Anglo-Saxon iconography was the construction of Stainborough Castle – nearly the first mock castle of eighteenth-century landscape design. It was preceded only by

The keep at Stainborough Castle – one of the first landscape structures of the eighteenth-century Gothic Revival.

Part of the curtain walling of Stainborough Castle – clearly showing the Gothic features to be repeated at both Steeple Lodge and the Hawking Tower.

Alfred's Hall in Cirencester Park, designed by his cousin, Lord Bathurst, with Alexander Pope, and built in 1721. This is the first of many parallels between Cirencester and the Wentworths' estates at Wentworth Castle and Boughton Park.

Gothic architecture was Anglo-Saxon and the Anglo-Saxon was the lineal ancestor of the Jacobite as opposed to the Hanoverian. The Gothic architectural revival appealed to Tory Jacobite sympathisers as well as to the Whigs who adopted this iconography to naturalise the Hanoverian dynasty so that they were no longer perceived as foreign.[6] This movement culminated in the 1836 decision to rebuild the Houses of Parliament in a Gothic style.

Thomas Wentworth passed away at Wentworth Castle on 15 November 1739, leaving a son, William, and three daughters. William Wentworth, the second Earl of the second creation, was only 18 when his father died and spent two of his remaining minor years in Italy before coming into his inheritance and marrying Anne, second daughter and heiress of the Duke of

Argyll. Her appearance was warmly praised by Horace Walpole in his 1746 poem, "The Beauties".[7]

William Wentworth was a man content to eschew public life. He inherited his father's passion for landscape structures and follies. Both Wentworth Castle and Boughton Park still bear witness to this enthusiasm. Although William Wentworth softened and naturalised his father's geometric garden designs, his interest lay more in the aesthetic architectural contribution that structures could make to the landscape, rather than in any clandestine political statement. He was an innovative dilettante in Gothic architecture – usually a guarantee of first-class follies!

William Wentworth is recognised as being an amateur architect in his own right, being credited with the design of the impressive Palladian southeast wing at Wentworth Castle, added between 1759 and 1764. Lord Verulam wrote in 1768 that "Lord Strafford himself is his own architect and contriver in everything",[8] whilst Lord Wharncliffe described him as "eminently skilled in architecture and virtue."[9] This is confirmed by his great friend Horace Walpole and by William Bray. William Wentworth is credited with the actual design of the Obelisk at Boughton, and may well have been responsible for the design of the other landscape structures at his Northamptonshire estate. As Horace Walpole wrote: "In general it is probably true, that the possessor, if he has any taste, must be the best designer of his own improvements. He sees his situation in all seasons of the year, at all times of the day. He knows where beauty will not clash with convenience, and observes in his silent walks or accidental rides a thousand hints that must escape a person who in a few days sketches out a pretty picture, but has not had leisure to examine the details and relations of every part."[10]

The majority of William Wentworth's architectural flights of fancy at Boughton still exist today in their original form. Indeed, it is still possible to look across this tranquil valley of Boughton Park to see the follies in their original setting, unspoilt by the onset of the twentieth century. England's heritage has, without doubt, been enriched by such landed eccentrics who could indulge their whims by building such structures.

William Wentworth, second Earl Strafford of the second creation (1722–91), who ornamented Boughton Park with follies and other landscape structures. From a mezzotint after Reynolds.
(Courtesy: Northern College)

William Wentworth died of the stone, without an heir, on 10 March 1791. He was buried on 26 March, alongside his father in the family vault beneath the Wentworth Chapel at the Church of St George of England, Toddington, Bedfordshire.

William Wentworth's estates were inherited by his three sisters – Anne, Lucy and Henrietta – as tenants-in-common. However, as they were anxious to hold their shares in severalty they obtained an Act of Parliament in 1795 by which the Boughton and Pitsford estates were assigned to Richard William Howard-Vyse, a minor, son of General Richard Vyse and Anne, daughter and heiress of Lucy Wentworth and Sir George Howard. In this way the estate remained, to all intents and purposes, in the same family from 1717 to 1927 – a period of 210 years. The Boughton and Pitsford estates were finally broken up and sold by Sir Richard Granville Hylton Howard-Vyse, the last Lord of the Manor.

The Church of St George of England, Toddington, Bedfordshire. The Wentworth Chapel is on the left.

Simplified Wentworth/Howard-Vyse family tree

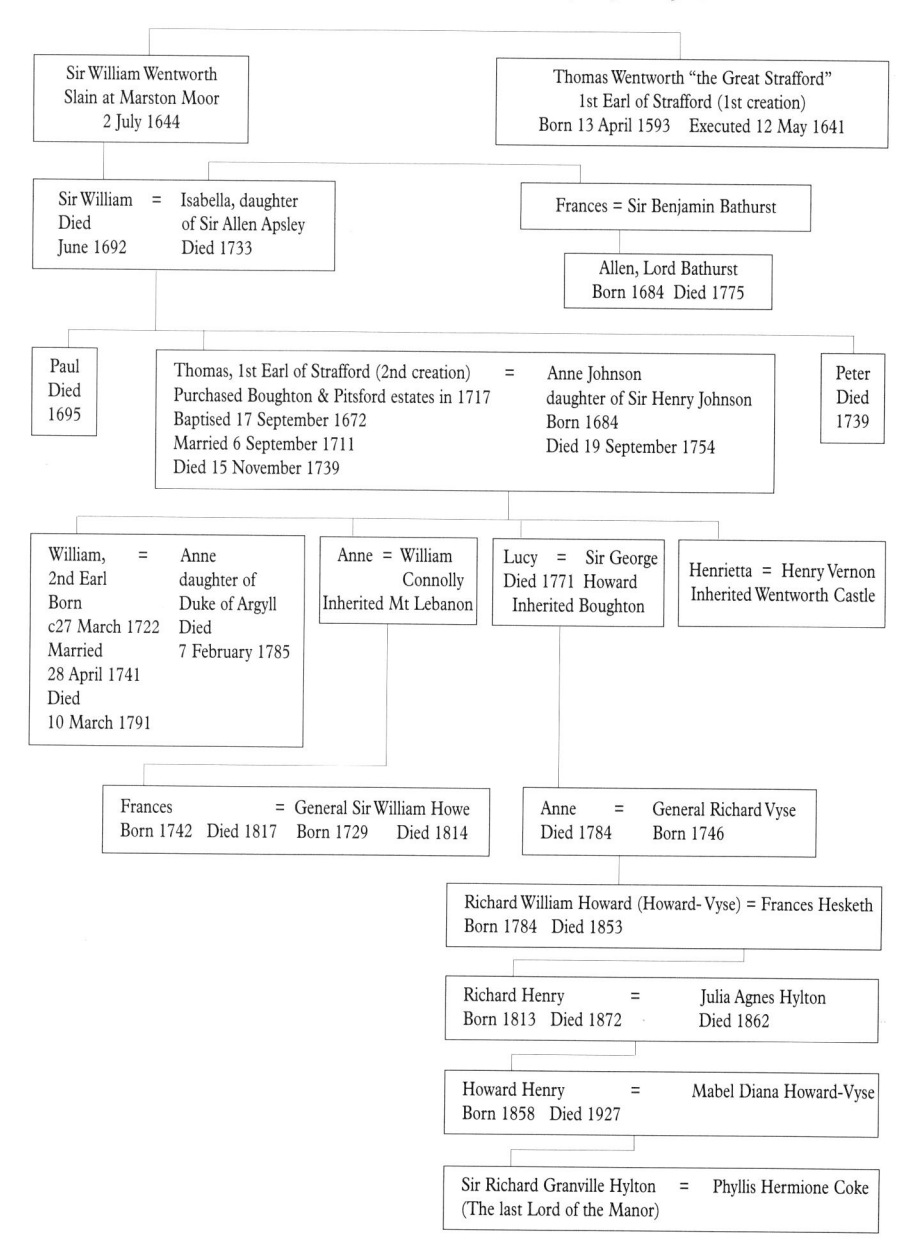

- **Sir William Wentworth**
  Slain at Marston Moor
  2 July 1644

  - **Sir William** = **Isabella, daughter of Sir Allen Apsley**
    Died June 1692   Died 1733

    - **Paul** Died 1695
    - **Thomas, 1st Earl of Strafford (2nd creation)** = **Anne Johnson**
      Purchased Boughton & Pitsford estates in 1717   daughter of Sir Henry Johnson
      Baptised 17 September 1672   Born 1684
      Married 6 September 1711   Died 19 September 1754
      Died 15 November 1739
    - **Peter** Died 1739

      - **William, 2nd Earl** = **Anne daughter of Duke of Argyll**
        Born c27 March 1722   Died 7 February 1785
        Married 28 April 1741
        Died 10 March 1791
      - **Anne** = **William Connolly**
        Inherited Mt Lebanon
      - **Lucy** = **Sir George Howard**
        Died 1771   Inherited Boughton
      - **Henrietta** = **Henry Vernon**
        Inherited Wentworth Castle

        - **Frances** = **General Sir William Howe**
          Born 1742 Died 1817   Born 1729 Died 1814
        - **Anne** = **General Richard Vyse**
          Died 1784   Born 1746

          - **Richard William Howard (Howard-Vyse)** = **Frances Hesketh**
            Born 1784 Died 1853

            - **Richard Henry** = **Julia Agnes Hylton**
              Born 1813 Died 1872   Died 1862

              - **Howard Henry** = **Mabel Diana Howard-Vyse**
                Born 1858 Died 1927

                - **Sir Richard Granville Hylton** = **Phyllis Hermione Coke**
                  (The last Lord of the Manor)

- **Thomas Wentworth "the Great Strafford"**
  1st Earl of Strafford (1st creation)
  Born 13 April 1593   Executed 12 May 1641

  - **Frances** = **Sir Benjamin Bathurst**

    - **Allen, Lord Bathurst**
      Born 1684 Died 1775

HORACE WALPOLE
and other influences

"Horace Walpole set a fashion in Gothic architecture as well as in Gothic literature. In 1750 he rebuilt his house at Strawberry Hill in the Gothic style; and within a few years it had become fashionable for gentlemen to embellish their houses with Gothic facades and their gardens with Gothic ruins. Other excursions into the exotic, such as...imitation grottoes...took their place alongside sham castles and summerhouses...By the 1790s...it was an integral part of the Romantic Movement, that immensely important complex of ideas which was to transform the whole of European thought within little more than a generation."[1]

Horace Walpole (1717–97), christened Horatio, was the youngest child by 11 years of Sir Robert Walpole, generally credited as England's first Prime Minister. The self-appointed arbiter of the national taste, Horace Walpole chronicled the social and political history of his age, was a pivotal influence on architecture and landscape design, and a tireless visitor to country seats. He was brought up at the splendid Palladian house of Houghton in Norfolk.

Horace Walpole (1717–97), a close friend and regular correspondent of William Wentworth. This previously unrecorded portrait miniature is by Pompeo Batoni.
(Courtesy: Bonhams)

Horace Walpole was the greatest of the eighteenth-century Gothic Revivalists. He partly designed and had built the first completely Gothic house of the Revival, Strawberry Hill, in Twickenham. Complete with a tower, battlements, pinnacles and quatrefoil windows, the main construction started in 1750. Walpole is also credited with the invention of a new genre of Romantic literature, the Gothic novel; his *The Castle of Otranto* was published

Horace Walpole's Strawberry Hill – the first completely Gothic house of the Revival. Note the similarities with Bunkers Hill Farm.

in 1764. So successful was the novel that it was reprinted six times within Walpole's lifetime and is still in print today.

A small, frail man of literary tastes, with a penchant for collecting, Horace Walpole noted that asymmetry of design should become a central principle of Gothic landscape design and structure. He once remarked that one needed taste to appreciate classical art but passion to appreciate the Gothic.

Walpole was a close friend and regular correspondent of William Wentworth, second Earl of Strafford. Indeed, in 1769, Walpole wrote to William Wentworth: "When you have been so constantly good to me, my good Lord, without changing, do you wonder that our friendship has lasted so long?...we have seen friendships without number born and die. Ours was not formed on interest, nor alliance; and politics, the poison of all English connections, never entered into ours."[2]

Like William Wentworth, Horace Walpole had no real appetite for the political scene. Instead, he cultivated an impressive circle of friends and acquaintances with whom he carried on a voluminous correspondence. Indeed, his letters – now published in more than 40 volumes – are among the classics of English writing.

The first mention of the Wentworths socialising with Horace Walpole occurs just after Sir Robert Walpole's fall from power in 1742, when the Wentworths showed their affection by promptly asking him to dinner. However, there is evidence of a much earlier childhood friendship for, in December 1730, at the age of only eight, William Wentworth wrote to his father that "Master Wallpole came to me last night, we playd at Quadarill and I won 10 pence at a penny a fish."[3]

Their friendship was to last a lifetime. Even in his will William Wentworth remembered him: "I leave to Horatio Walpole, son of the Earl of Orford that was minister to George 2nd...the sum of five hundred pounds...as a small mark of the happiness...[his] friendship gave me."[4] A considerable sum in the 1790s, equivalent to over £22,500 today.[5]

Walpole's cousin and close friend, Field Marshal Henry Seymour Conway, was another beneficiary of William Wentworth's will. Conway, apart from his military exploits, was also responsible for a variety of landscape structures at his Park Place residence in Berkshire – no doubt inspired by his cousin's ideas.

Walpole's correspondence to William Wentworth is considered, by the editor of his letters, to be "among the best he wrote".[6] William Wentworth inherited from his father Mount Lebanon, an impressive Twickenham residence on the banks of the Thames overlooking Eel Pie Island. Previously the residence of Dr William Fuller, a friend of Pepys, Mount Lebanon was purchased by Thomas Wentworth in 1701. Less than a mile from Walpole's Strawberry Hill, this property allowed William Wentworth to maintain a close relationship with Walpole's "Strawberry Committee", who so greatly influenced the Gothic Revival of this period.

On William Wentworth's death, Mount Lebanon went to his sister, Lady Anne Connolly, and therefore subsequently into the family of General Sir William Howe. The nephew of Howe's wife, Lady Frances, was Field Marshal Byng, for whom the title of Earl of Strafford was revived in 1847. Mount Lebanon was demolished in 1794 to make way for an even grander residence, to be occupied by Byng's sisters. Unfortunately, even that house has not survived; the only trace to be found today being a suburban street with the name "Lebanon Park".

Walpole's friendship with William Wentworth even extended to the design of at least one of his landscape structures, for in 1760 he wrote of "a Gothic building in the Menagerie [at Wentworth Castle], proposed by me and drawn by Mr Bentley...built by this Lord."[7]

Wentworth Castle obviously impressed Horace Walpole, for he wrote in 1770: "If a model is sought of the most perfect taste in architecture, where grace softens dignity, and lightness attempers magnificence; where proportion removes every part from peculiar observation, and delicacy of execution recalls every part to notice; where the position is the most happy, and even the colour of the stone the most harmonious; the virtuoso should be directed to the new front [designed by William Wentworth] of Wentworth-castle: the result of the same elegant judgement that had before distributed so many beauties over the domain, and called from wood, water, hills, prospects and buildings, a compendium of picturesque nature, improved by the chastity of art."[8]

Horace Walpole had previously given perhaps the ultimate compliment to William Wentworth when he wrote in 1756 that "Nobody has a truer taste than Lord Strafford",[9] confirming this in 1768, writing: "Nobody has better taste than this Lord"[10] – a hearty endorsement of the work and architectural designs instigated by William Wentworth.

Mention has already been made of the very early Gothic Revival structure named Alfred's Hall in Cirencester Park, Gloucestershire, designed by Thomas Wentworth's cousin, Allen, first Earl of Bathurst, (1684–1775), with Alexander Pope. Bathurst was a cheerful man, a Tory with Jacobite leanings and a good friend of Alexander Pope with whom he shared a passion for landscape design and silviculture.

The present Earl Bathurst believes that "with the dates and their interests – the first Earl Bathurst was very sympathetic to the Jacobites if not one in fact – it is surely more than likely that they compared notes about their plans and ideas to bring back the Norman style to their park buildings? Earl Bathurst was also his own architect together with the advice of Alexander Pope."[11]

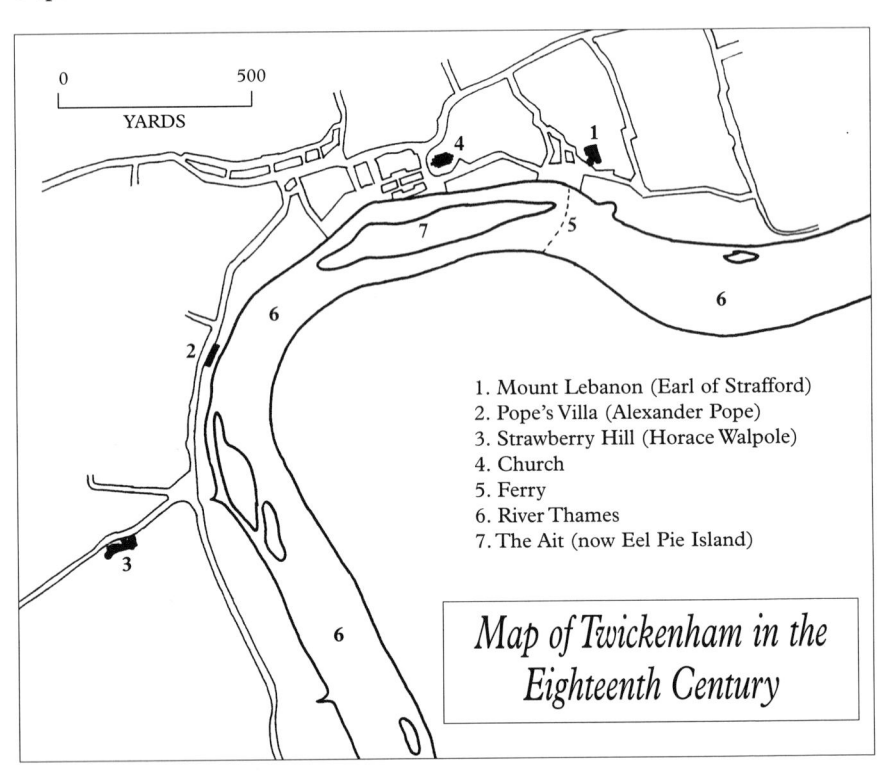

1. Mount Lebanon (Earl of Strafford)
2. Pope's Villa (Alexander Pope)
3. Strawberry Hill (Horace Walpole)
4. Church
5. Ferry
6. River Thames
7. The Ait (now Eel Pie Island)

Map of Twickenham in the Eighteenth Century

If anything, this is a conservative interpretation of the evidence. Bathurst, like Thomas Wentworth, had been elevated to the peerage by the Tory government of Queen Anne in response to an immediate tactical need for more Tory peers. Stainborough Castle might well have been directly inspired by Bathurst's building of Alfred's Hall. Structures such as the Ivy Lodge at Cirencester Park share a common style with those at Boughton. Bathurst was even the sole executor for the will of Thomas Wentworth's wife.

Bathurst was a frequent correspondent with his cousin, Thomas Wentworth, often discussing landscaping schemes, including Boughton Park. Indeed, he wrote that "I have almost a mind to make a journey on purpose to see this place [Boughton] to try if I can't lay a scheme of making itt convenient and habitable."[12] Typical of this regular correspondence is a letter from Bathurst dated 6 September 1736 which discusses his plans for Cirencester before continuing: "I waited upon my Lord Chancellor a little time ago who has a pretty place about 12 miles off, but a sad house and finds himself obliged to build. ...he is so surrounded with Comon fields that I think he cant possibly make a great thing of it, but it may be made a pretty thing. Ye park may be made like yours at Boughton."[13] Earlier, in 1732, Bathurst had written: "I delight in the...building of the Castle [Stainborough Castle at Wentworth] tho is neither Egyptian or Grecian but of a more proper order, the Saxon."[14]

Alexander Pope (1688–1744), the renowned satirical poet, was an even closer neighbour to Thomas Wentworth in Twickenham than William Wentworth to Horace Walpole, living there from 1719 to 1744. Correspondence in 1725 between the Duke of Bedford and Thomas Wentworth shows that Pope and Wentworth were well acquainted, for the Duke of Bedford writes: "I beg you will bring Mr Pope with you, or in case he should have left you by this time that you would be so kind as to write to him to meet you there [at Woburn]."[15] Some days later, the Duke of Bedford writes that Pope's "Expression of the Honour he has for your Lordship [Thomas Wentworth] and the value he puts upon your Favour give me a greater esteem for him and a greater Opinion of his Judgement than all his other writings besides."[16] Alfred's Hall was remodelled with Pope's advice in 1732, thereby anticipating the most celebrated ruin designer of them all, Sanderson Miller. As the reader will see later, William Wentworth used an extract from Pope's philosophical poem *An Essay on Man* for the inscription on the Obelisk at Boughton.

Sanderson Miller (1716–80), a country gentleman and amateur architect, was a key figure in promoting an historical if sentimental awareness of the mediaeval past and in translating that awareness to buildings set in landscapes – including Edgehill, Hagley Hall and Wroxton Abbey. To some extent he was a rival of Horace Walpole who, despite some barbed comments, could be praising as with his celebrated comment that "There is a ruined castle [at Hagley Hall] built by Miller, that would get him the freedom even of Strawberry, it has the true rust of the Barons' Wars."[17] Sanderson Miller's influence on the design of the Spectacle at Boughton is detailed later.

Both Thomas and, in particular, William Wentworth were therefore at the very heart of the Gothic Revival movement during the eighteenth century. Their close friends included some of the most influential figures in the movement and this is reflected in the landscapes created by the Wentworths at both Boughton Park and Wentworth Castle. In effect, the design of our English landscape was enhanced by a group of talented amateur enthusiasts, intent on recreating an idealistic version of Gothic England on their country estates. As Alexander Pope wrote to Thomas Wentworth: "I have long been convinced that neither Acres, nor Wise; nor any publick Professors of Gardening, (any more than any publick Professors of Virtue) are equal to the Private Practisers of it."[18] Boughton Park today is a fine testimony to the vision, passion and ability of the "Private Practisers".

BOUGHTON HALL

Ground plans for the original Boughton Hall show a great hall with a screens passage dividing the entrance from the Hall itself, a musicians' gallery, and a large fireplace on the east wall. All these features indicate a late mediaeval origin. The Green family, who bought the estate in 1340, may well have been the builders.[1]

Thomas Badeslade (c1715–1750), a mapmaker and topographical draughtsman, was privately commissioned by Thomas Wentworth to make a drawing of the house and park in 1732. It is a bird's-eye view, and shows the layout of the garden as well. The main entrance and drive seem to be in roughly the same position as they are today. The house had a central block facing west, with wings projecting from the west side. There was an entrance archway in the north wing, which was two storeys high, with dormer windows for the attics. The south wing was three storeys high, with two wide projecting bays. This wing was probably added in the sixteenth century. To the east of the house lay a range of outbuildings, including a circular pigeon house. To the north can be seen the bowling green, now the cricket pitch, where Charles I played during his imprisonment at nearby Holdenby House from 16 February to 4 June 1647. The gardens were formal in layout, with trimmed hedges and walks, typical of the type of garden design for the period. Badeslade later made a similar study of Wentworth Castle in 1739.

Thomas Wentworth probably first learnt of Boughton Hall from his brother Peter who was, in 1713, actively looking for a Northamptonshire seat for his brother which "may be your half way house into Yorkshire."[2] However, it was not until 1717 that Thomas Wentworth finally purchased the Boughton and Pitsford estates from Lord Ashburnham for £9,000, soon after the case for impeachment against him floundered. By this time, the house and grounds had been neglected, prompting Lord Bathurst to write that he was "sorry to find...that your house at Boughton is so indifferent;...[with] the gardens being a little run to ruin."[3] By 1719, Thomas Wentworth had obviously made Boughton far more agreeable by works including "puling downe the wals and other Work at the house",[4] occupying ten people for up to ten weeks, "Pointing ye Slatting"[5] and "Plastering work in ye Rooms".[6] This prompted the same Lord Bathurst to write, in 1719: "I passed by Boughton and show'd it to Mr Lewis and described itt's beauties, and he is much charm'd with itt."[7] Today, there are still significant remains of the formal garden and wilderness, including a remarkable viewing terrace, ha-ha and a number of original yews and hollies.

According to the *Boughton Parish Magazine*, "the old Hall...stood facing the elm avenue, between the present outbuildings and the kitchen garden, the walls of which and two gateways leading into the village are the only trace remaining of the house and its precincts."[8] However, by examining the Badeslade drawing of 1732 and evidence to be seen in the garden today, I would conjecture that it is far more likely that the old Boughton Hall stood, not on the site of the cricket pitch as is commonly believed, but in roughly the same position as the present Hall but with the front facing almost due west towards the Northampton to Market Harborough road.

John Bridges, one of the first historians of the county, stated that "The Manor House or seat of the Earl of Strafford is old but not large. It is pleasantly situated upon a rising ground which commands a very extensive prospect. The gardens and woods adjoining it are well disposed."[9]

One anonymous late eighteenth-century visitor to Boughton Hall gives a more detailed account, as follows: "The house fronts the road on our right, and is but a small distance from it, tho' it is only seen at the bottom of two or three vistas, thro' which its white battlements have a very picturesque effect. We entered the gates beyond to examine the inside of this ancient seat, and were much gratified.

"...From our own inspection of the house, which is small, we found it built in the form of a half H, with gables, which the present possessor, Lord

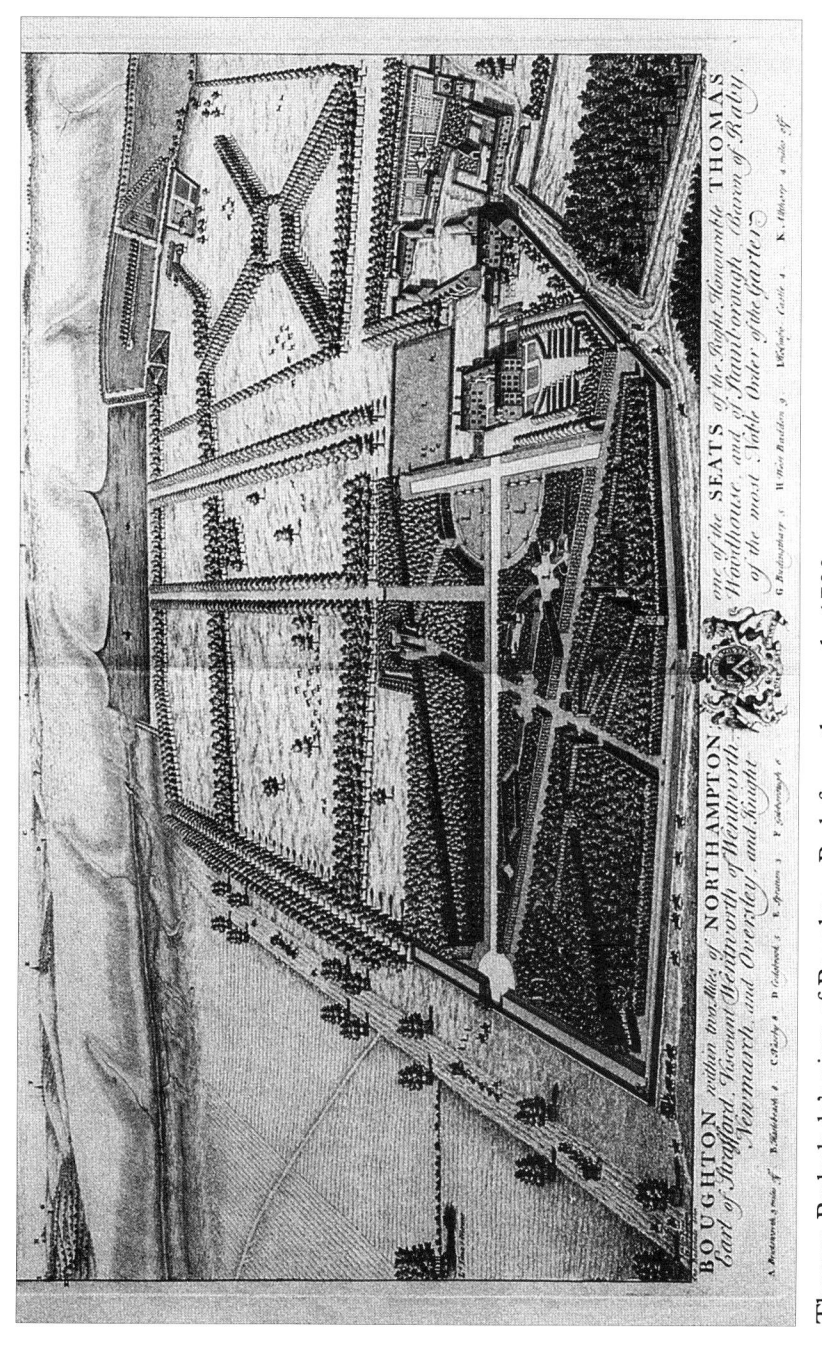

Thomas Badeslade's view of Boughton Park from the south, 1732.
(Courtesy: Northamptonshire Libraries)

Strafford, has carried up into battlements, and turrets, so as to have a very picturesque effect. We entered at the side, thro' a passage into an ancient hall, with a screen. This respectable old room is lofty, and the windows high, quite in the ancient style. Here hung a picture of the famous Lord Strafford and his dog, probably a copy of that at Stainborough, the principal seat of the family, in Yorkshire. We next entered the area of the stair case; on the right of which is a small dining room and billiard room. The stair case, which is of massy wooden rails, led us to the drawing room, and a few other comfortable apartments. The study we saw in the opposite wing.

"The whole house is indeed but small; but exhibits sufficient to convey ideas of happy retirement. The luxuriant ivy which covers altogether the back of the house, and spreads over one tower of the front; the perfect union of the whole, both in size and ornament..."[10]

About 1795 George Baker made a sketch of the house, which he later published in his *History of Northamptonshire*.[11] This shows the alterations made by William Wentworth including the roofline with battlements and towers. The battlements which William Wentworth built on to it may account for the village tradition that there is the site of a castle in the grounds of Boughton Hall.

George Baker's sketch of Boughton Hall, c1795, showing the Gothic battlements and towers added by William Wentworth.

As the reader will see from the following pages, William Wentworth's building activities were not confined to the house alone. He was a friend of Horace Walpole, who popularised the eighteenth-century version of mediaeval architecture sometimes referred to as "Gothick". The remaining examples of William Wentworth's work show him to have followed his friend in the use of this style for the folly structures around Boughton.

The house was occupied by the Earl of Ross for a short time after William Wentworth's death and subsequently became a rendezvous for the Pytchley Hunt while under the management of John Warde, who was the last occupier of Boughton Hall until his departure in 1808. In 1809 the Howard-Vyse family contemplated alterations to the house, commissioning Luke Kirshaw of Northampton to design them. The whole work was rather Gothic in character, but nothing appears to have been done and the house was left to decay. "The old building had...fallen utterly to ruins. Neither Lady Lucy Howard, Sir George Howard nor their grandson had taken much interest in the place, which had been left in the care of an agent named Buckland. He let the place fall into rack and ruin and then absconded and shot himself."[12] By 1822 the site was nearly levelled to the ground. The present house was built in 1844, the architect being Richard Burn.

BOUGHTON PARK

On 31 October 1994, English Heritage included Boughton Park on their *Register of Parks and Gardens of Special Historic Interest in England* as a Grade II site. Northamptonshire, as a county, has only 23 such sites, eight in all being in Daventry District. The other seven sites are Althorp (I), Canons Ashby (II★), Holdenby (II★), The Manor House, Ashby St Ledgers (II), Cottesbrooke Hall (II), Fawsley (II) and Lamport Hall (II). But what of the history of Boughton Park, now that it has been recognised as being of national importance?

David Jacques, Chairman of the Garden and Landscapes Committee for the International Council on Monuments and Sites, believes: "Strafford does not seem to have made a conventional park such as ['Capability'] Brown would have done. Instead of the removal of hedgerows and the insertion of classical temples to give the character of Greek or Roman antiquity, here is an attempt to recover the character of the mediaeval English countryside (as Strafford would have understood it) by adding Gothic ornamentation to existing and new building. The same theme can be seen at Badminton, Eridge, Hagley and other places, and quite likely Boughton is the product of Strafford's close friendship with Horace Walpole."[1]

Detailed accounts exist of work carried out for Thomas Wentworth in the garden and park at Boughton. Once Thomas Wentworth had purchased the estate in 1717, work seems to have begun almost immediately to transform the gardens described by Lord Bathurst as "a little run to ruin".[2] Strafford's agent writes on 24 October 1717, that "att Boughton...all is att quiet, tho Gardners are digging and planting".[3] During 1718, payments are recorded for "6 thousand 5 hundred plants for the...parck"[4] and for "repairing the mound walls".[5] The mound is probably Lord Vaux's Mount, named after a previous owner of Boughton Hall, as shown on Badeslade's drawing and is described by the Royal Commission on Historic Monuments: "The mound, which stands on the N. edge of the field, is tree covered...The mound is 2.2 m high and 15 m in diameter and no ditch is visible."[6] Sherds from a Neolithic or Bronze Age vessel have been found nearby. It is shown on Ordnance Survey maps as a tumulus (Ordnance Survey reference SP 747659).

Although Lord Bathurst states in 1717 that Boughton has "Fine groves and large rows of old elms in a fine country",[7] more ambitious work is deemed essential in 1721 when Edward Briggs, presumably in a role equivalent to a Head Gardener, writes to ask "your Lordship [where] to have the rest of the Elms planted...[perhaps] the garden and the old walks in ye park:- your Lordship was pleased to tell me once when I had trees I should plant a walk a cross ye bottom of yr Park Betwixt ye Cornor whore ye Bridge is and yc Bottom of yr Great Walk that gaze from yr Boulinggreen:- one Line to Line with ye two Lowest trees of the two walks and the other Line Below it...and please your Lordship there will not be trees a noff to plant it at :20: foot a part nor at :22: foot a part But if your Lordship pleases to let me plant them :36: foot a part: they will Showe a walk and Look well and if your Lordship please at affter to put a tree in Betwixt them...in two or three years time they will be :18: foot a part which is a very Good Distance for a Elme."[8]

Work obviously proceeds at a pace for, just two weeks later, Briggs writes that "I have planted yr...finest sized Elms...it Looks very well and I hope it will please your Lordship when your Lordship Coms...I have planted all yr old wants in walk for yr park:- all But that walk that your Lordship speaks of."[9]

Thomas Wentworth evidently visits Boughton at this point for Briggs' next letter only two weeks later says: "I am Glad that your Lordship liks...yr Mount", going on to say that he has acquired additional trees for the park: "the Elms that is at Moulton I think it is proper to put them In yr Cros Walk if your Lordship pleases."[10] The elm planting by the lake, the "Cros Walk" and the Mount (in the garden, not the Lord Vaux's Mount referred to

Map of Boughton Park c1790

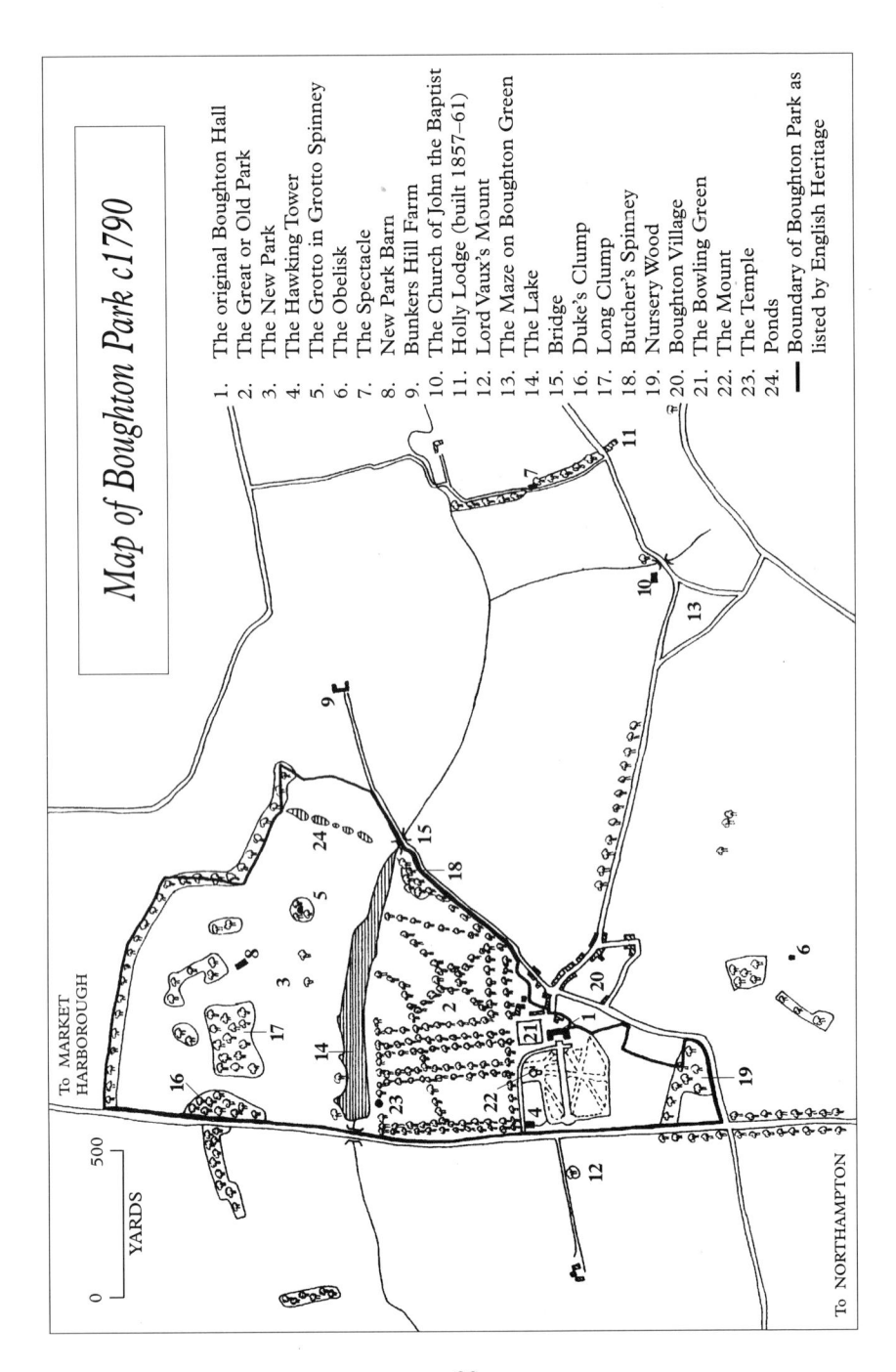

1. The original Boughton Hall
2. The Great or Old Park
3. The New Park
4. The Hawking Tower
5. The Grotto in Grotto Spinney
6. The Obelisk
7. The Spectacle
8. New Park Barn
9. Bunkers Hill Farm
10. The Church of John the Baptist
11. Holly Lodge (built 1857–61)
12. Lord Vaux's Mount
13. The Maze on Boughton Green
14. The Lake
15. Bridge
16. Duke's Clump
17. Long Clump
18. Butcher's Spinney
19. Nursery Wood
20. Boughton Village
21. The Bowling Green
22. The Mount
23. The Temple
24. Ponds

— Boundary of Boughton Park as listed by English Heritage

Map of Boughton Park today

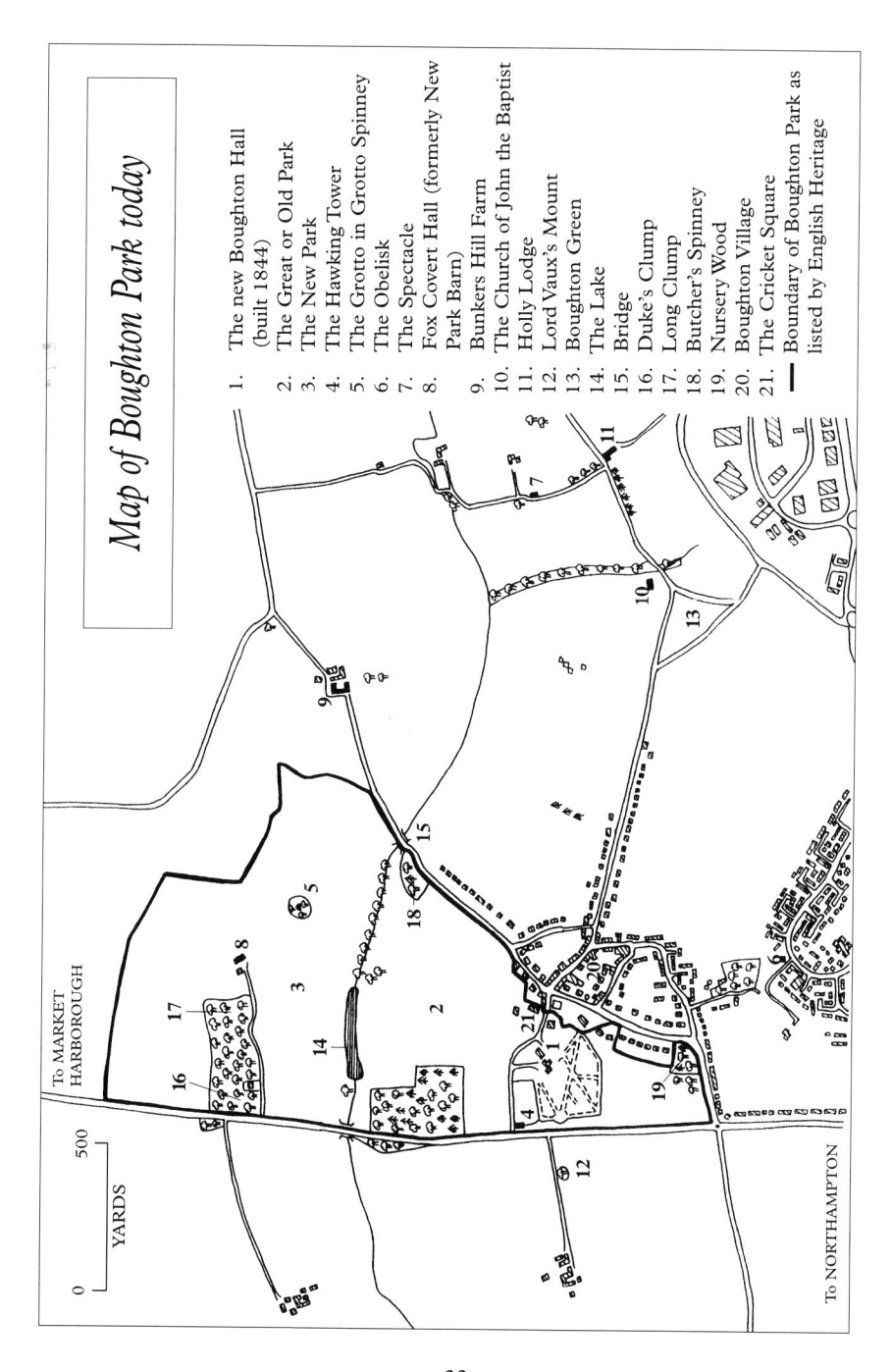

1. The new Boughton Hall (built 1844)
2. The Great or Old Park
3. The New Park
4. The Hawking Tower
5. The Grotto in Grotto Spinney
6. The Obelisk
7. The Spectacle
8. Fox Covert Hall (formerly New Park Barn)
9. Bunkers Hill Farm
10. The Church of John the Baptist
11. Holly Lodge
12. Lord Vaux's Mount
13. Boughton Green
14. The Lake
15. Bridge
16. Duke's Clump
17. Long Clump
18. Butcher's Spinney
19. Nursery Wood
20. Boughton Village
21. The Cricket Square
— Boundary of Boughton Park as listed by English Heritage

previously) are all clearly shown on Badeslade's 1732 drawing.

In January 1721, Briggs writes "to give your Lordship an account that the 2 men has all most finnist the Mount and I Desrire of your Lordship to know Wither your Lordship will have the Slops of yr Mount turfft or No. I think and please your Lordship it will be very proper for to have it turfft: for it is stons and low Earth will wash a way before it turfft...and turffing will hould it up at once."[11]

Planting schemes, however, are still proceeding, for Briggs writes that "We have made preparation for planting the Hornbeame...theire wants about 13:- or :14 Elms for to make up what is wanting in yr walks in yr park...we have gott some...plants from yr wood...and we are planting them in yr wilderness."[12] He also writes that "I have Raised :61: Horschessnutts Last Night and we are a going to plant ye :17 at yr Ponds whoar your Lordship ordered."[13]

The next series of letters, dating from 1732, are perhaps some of the most historically interesting as they chronicle the work of Thomas Badeslade, the renowned mapmaker and topographical draughtsman, at Boughton. Surviving letters recording his methods of working and the difficulties he encountered are, I understand, particularly rare.

Writing from Exton on 16 January 1732, Badeslade states that "I shall gladly serve Your Lordship at Your own terms, and survey the Land and Gardens of Boughton as soon as weather permits, but I cannot stand to take the angles while its so cold nor make the survey correctly; and if it should continue to snow I cant measure at all. I will be best therfore to stay 'till the Days are longer, and ill finish the map in March, which is perhaps as soon as I could do if I was to begin now. And I am as yet finishing the Maps of Ld Gainsboroughs Serveys."[14]

After visiting Boughton, Badeslade writes to Thomas Wentworth: "I believe you will judge best by the map of the Gardens and Park which Prospect will do best for a Print. It will be done by the larger scale and most distinct if taken from the South looking Northward, the Gardens will then pocess the whole width of the Paper and succeeded by the Park...If taken from the Road & looking Eastward the Park must come on the side of the Gardens into the width of the Paper which will occasion the Gardens to be Drawn very small, but taken this way the draught will be phaps best understood – But to make it quite picturess as likely Your Lordship would chuse to saw the old Church and...Boughton Fair in the Fore Ground, and then drawing the Village Gardens and Park...with the fine landscape westward. But here will be so many figures."[15]

As can be seen from the Badeslade drawing reproduced on page 27, it is the first of these options that Thomas Wentworth chose. At the end of May 1732, Badeslade is able to report that "With much difficulty I have finished the Rough Draught of the Survey of Boughton after two months labour, and to make the fair draft will take as much time more."[16] The finished drawing provides a superb view of Boughton before William Wentworth began to build his Gothic follies and enlarge the park.

With such a large estate, work is always in progress. In June 1737 John Worley, Thomas Wentworth's steward, writes: "Briggs had a man into the Gardens...They have Gotten the Gardens in a Good forwardness."[17] However, although a long-term employee of the Wentworths at Boughton, Briggs was not without his faults, as Worley points out in this wryly amusing extract, also from June 1737: "Yesterday Briggs was with me & made Hevey Complaining which he hath done several Times Before; for a man but I Often finding Mr Whitfield and him at Nixons. Told him I durst not Ask my Lord for a man while he had Time to Goo to ye Alehouse so much."[18]

One of the illustrious visitors to Boughton was a Hungarian aristocrat, Count Ferenc Széchényi, (1754–1820), who visited England in 1787. His travel diary shows that his main interests were in social life and economic conditions as he believed these would be beneficial to his country. In England his attention turned to parks and gardens, including Boughton, which he visited in September, writing that: " The building follows the old taste, is not especially furnished, it is not remarkable for pictures or other objects of art...yet it offers exciting vistas through the alleys that pass through the garden. The garden is small, but lovely; the place with the most beautiful view

Ha-ha walls are a feature of Boughton Park.

over the remote meadows and hills is on the highway side. From this and from the park the house is separated by a wall sunk in a ditch, which is imperceptable from a distance...Not far from the place where one can enter the park and drive to the house there is a look-out tower. The Earl spends four months in the town, two months here, the other six...in Yorkshire, and loves solitude!"[19]

An anonymous traveller of a similar period shared Count Széchényi's enthusiasm, stating that "the broken grounds; with rich trees and pleasing vistas, (for *vistas* here are *pleasing*) afforded us a short visit of soothing delight."[20]

Arthur Young, in 1771, during one of his tours, mentions that "Near Northampton the Earl of Strafford has a seat, the gardens finely situated: they are ornamented with several temples in a very light and elegant stile. The grounds are well wooded."[21]

The full extent of Boughton Park is a matter for some debate, the area listed by English Heritage being, in effect, the area of the more formal park. This comprised three main areas: the gardens, the Great or Old Park and the

The Howard-Vyse map of Boughton Park in 1794. Features to note include: the formal gardens of the old Hall; the lines of trees in the park; the lake at the bottom of the valley stretching from the Market Harborough Road to Butcher's Lane; and the woods of Duke's Clump, Fox Covert, Grotto Spinney and Butcher's Spinney.
(Courtesy: Northampton Record Office)

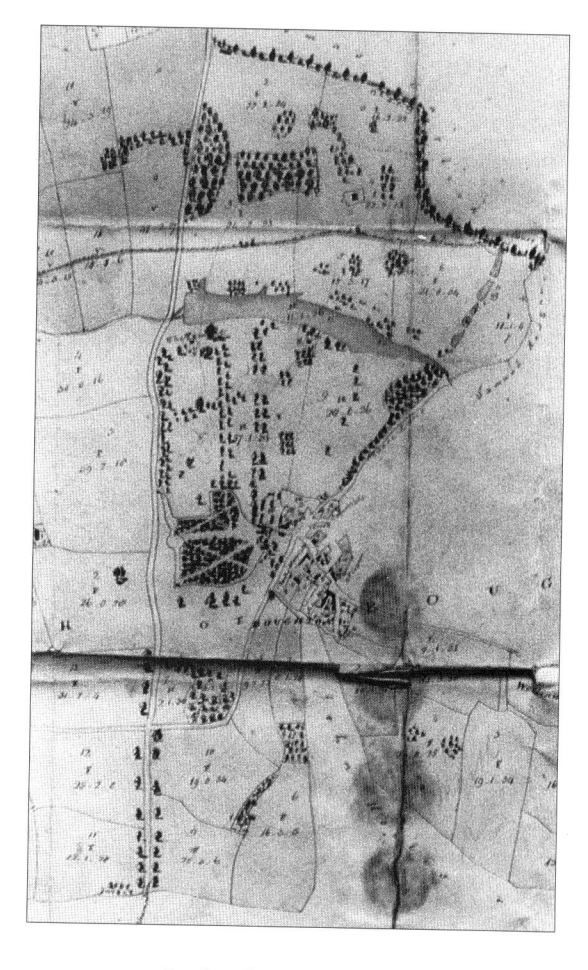

New Park. Mistakenly, on some maps, only the Great or Old Park is shown. This is the area bounded by the Northampton to Market Harborough Road to the west, the gardens of Boughton Hall to the south, Butcher's Lane to the east and the lake at the bottom of the valley to the north. The New Park includes the land on the Pitsford side of the valley, also bounded on the west by the Northampton to Market Harborough Road, the lake to the south, and northwards beyond the woods at Duke's Clump and Long Clump. This can clearly be seen on the 1794 estate map.[22] Other evidence includes Baker referring to "the grotto spring in the Park"[23] and, perhaps even more obviously, the name of Strafford's fortified barn to the northern side of the valley – New Park Barn. There are also documents c1798 which refer to John Warde leasing "the Great or Old Park" containing some 100 acres, and the "New Park" and plantations of about 124 acres.[24] The *Camden Britannia*, 1789 edition, also clearly shows Boughton Park extending north of the lake nearly to Pitsford as does a map of 1779 published by William Faden.[25] William Wentworth himself refers to his "house at Boughton in Northamptonshire with the offices, Gardens & parks on both sides the pond."[26]

Unfortunately, the 1794 estate map was drawn immediately after William Wentworth's death and so excludes the land he owned to the east of Butcher's Lane and around Bunkers Hill Farm as this he had bequeathed to his footman. By studying documents and by field walking it can be deduced that Bunkers Hill Farm would have formed part of a park that extended as far as Spectacle Lane. There is also strong evidence that the Spectacle formed part of the park boundary. It is positioned exactly on the Strafford estate boundary (now the Boughton/Moulton parish boundary); a band of trees including many elms were planted during Strafford's time between the Spectacle and Holly Lodge, and a sturdy stone wall was constructed on the same line. This is clearly shown on the 1794 estate map.

Of the eighteenth-century plantings on the northern side of the valley, Duke's Clump, Long Clump and Grotto Spinney survive. Considerable remnants of

The statue of Pegasus dates from c1725.

the original planting schemes for the Great or Old Park also survived until comparatively recently. "In the [18]80s...an avenue of elms extended from the...chapel through to the Green with not much space between them...many elms bordered the cricket ground. The park, with two well-defined avenues, was thickly wooded until a great gale in the [18]90s uprooted half the trees; time has further thinned them out."[27] Also surviving well into the twentieth century was a line of very old walnut trees leading directly to a statue of the flying horse, Pegasus, sited by the lake.

Believed to date from around 1725, Pegasus is first mentioned in documents of 1798 and, according to local folklore, is supposed to fly around the park at midnight when there is a special happening in the village. In 1968 it was restored and repositioned to the west of the Hall, near the Northampton to Market Harborough Road, where the original main entrance to Boughton Hall was located.

However, the principal and most important feature of the surviving eighteenth-century landscape at Boughton is the unique group of Grade II landscape structures and follies. It must always be remembered that they are a group and not simply a collection of individual structures. The design of Boughton Park, like other parks of its age and type, depends on the visual link between one structure and another, and the ability to travel in a direct line between them.

English Heritage emphasise that "A feature of the site is the set of gothic buildings which decorate the park and the wider landscape setting, focusing primarily on the valley to the north of the site. These formed a key part of the 2nd Earl's landscaping activities and, although several of them have not been included within the registered area, standing beyond the more formal park, their interconnection with the site is a highly important part of its character."[28]

By extending the park across the valley, William Wentworth was able to build these structures as eyecatchers on the horizon or on the brows of the surrounding hills; for example, Bunkers Hill Farm, New Park Barn, the Spectacle and the Obelisk. These were positioned at the visible or actual edge of the estate. They provide an exclamation mark in the language of landscape design, a place for the eye to rest at the end of a vista. Each relates to another. For example, if Strafford and his guests stood on his bowling green at Boughton Hall, they could have looked up to see Bunkers Hill Farm. They could then ride down one of the main avenues of trees, over the bridge at the bottom of the valley and, whilst riding, they would see the Spectacle and New Park Barn against the skyline. They could look back and see the Hawking Tower, and the castellated Boughton Hall and its outbuildings. In the distance they would be able to make out the Obelisk. A detour would be amusing for the Earl's guests as they watered their horses in "the Petrifying Spring" at the Grotto, hidden at the heart of Grotto Spinney.

Horace Walpole's account of a visit to nearby Stowe in 1770 provides both a first-hand account of how an ornamented park functioned at this time, and an insight into the social life of the period: "We breakfasted at half an hour after nine...then we walked in the garden, or drove about it in cabriolets, till it was time to dress; dined at three, which...lasted a great while...then again into the garden till past seven, when we came in, drank tea and coffee...You see there was a great sameness and little vivacity in all this. It was a little broken by fishing, and going round the park one of the mornings; but, in reality, the number of buildings and variety of scenes in the garden, made each day different from the rest, and my meditations on so historic a spot prevented my being tired. Every acre brings to one's mind...those that have inhabited, decorated, planned, or visited the place...On Wednesday night, a small Vauxhall was acted out for us at the Grotto in the Elysian fields, which was illuminated with lamps, as were the thicket and two little barks on the lake. With a little exaggeration, I could make you believe that nothing ever was so delightful."[29]

In a similar vein, William Wentworth would have been able to amuse both himself and his guests in his own idealised mediaeval landscape. It was his own world, a world he had created. And William Wentworth's world survives today, more than 200 years later in the tranquil valley of Boughton Park.

All the follies and other landscape structures within the area of Boughton Park are now described in chronological order.

The HAWKING TOWER

Ordnance Survey reference SP 748660

The Hawking Tower, a Grade II listed structure, stands as the entrance lodge to Boughton Hall on the main Northampton to Leicester road. Today it is used as a dwelling.

Built in the style of a church tower, the Hawking Tower is remarkably similar to Steeple Lodge at the Wentworths' seat of Wentworth Castle in South Yorkshire. Both are three storeys

The Hawking Tower.

Steeple Lodge at Wentworth Castle replicates the features of the Hawking Tower.

high with ogee-headed and quatrefoil windows, an outer staircase and a tower surmounted by battlements.

Until the 1930s there was, above the front door of the tower, a door accessible only by ladder to a loft room lined with nest boxes.[1] The mode of access to the upper storey is similar to that at New Park Barn.

Restoration and modernisation took place during the 1940s. It was during this period that, whilst installing a cesspit, the end of a mysterious tunnel was rediscovered.[2] It had previously been noted c1920, when Mr Harold Kimbell had been working within the grounds near to the driveway where it turns towards the present Boughton Hall.[3] Of brick construction and approximately four feet tall, the tunnel aligned roughly between the Hawking Tower and the former bowling green. More recent investigations to ascertain the precise location of the tunnel were abandoned as there was a danger of damaging the many services that are buried in the vicinity.

Local legends speak of there being a number of tunnels in the area, with this tunnel in particular being used to smuggle Charles I in and out of Boughton Hall. If this is true, then the tunnel must predate 1647, as there would not have been enough time for its construction during Charles I's relatively short imprisonment at nearby Holdenby. The existence of a tunnel could certainly have been of potential use to a prominent Jacobite conspirator such as Thomas Wentworth.

It is believed that the Hawking Tower is earlier than Steeple Lodge at Wentworth Castle, which dates from around 1775.[4] The Hawking Tower itself was built some time between 1739 and 1756. It is not shown on Badeslade's 1732 drawing and it is almost certainly the work of William Wentworth, who inherited the estate on his father's death in 1739, yet it is referred to by Horace Walpole in a letter to Strafford dated 28 August 1756: "I started at the vision of one of my own towers...I soon recollected that it must be Boughton."[5] This ambiguous wording has given rise to speculation that the design for the Hawking Tower was influenced by Walpole in much the same way that he helped design the Gothic summerhouse for Strafford at Wentworth Castle. It is more likely, however, to be a reference to Walpole's renowned Gothic residence of Strawberry Hill where Walpole had comparatively recently started major building works, including all manner of Gothic towers and castellations.

Another literary figure associated with the Hawking Tower is George John Whyte-Melville (1821–78). This nineteenth-century English novelist, who stayed at Boughton on numerous occasions, often used the Hawking Tower for his writing – no doubt inspired by the Gothic atmosphere created by William Wentworth. He published his first novel in 1853, although locally he is perhaps best known for his historical tale of old Northamptonshire – *Holmby House* – set at Holdenby, Althorpe and Boughton, the three great estates of the locality. This was published in 1860.

The Hawking Tower in 1835 by Edmund Gill showing the passing London to Derby coach. The gate piers with a lion and a griffin are clearly visible.
(Courtesy: Northamptonshire Libraries)

The raised situation of the Hawking Tower is due to the fact that the main road has been lowered by around 15 feet. The gate piers, of which only one now survives, originally bore stone figures of a lion and a griffin, heraldic supporters of the Earls of Strafford, holding shields bearing coats of arms. These had previously been located, as Badeslade's drawing shows, on gate piers at the original main entranceway where the statue of Pegasus now stands.

The lion and griffin have now been restored to the Boughton Estate, where they are positioned on another gateway, leading from the Hall to Boughton village. This gateway originally incorporated a castellated arch in the "Gothick" taste. Very similar in style to the archway leading into Home Farm at Wentworth Castle, the Boughton archway was considered structurally unsafe and removed around 20 years ago. Castellated walls, flanking this entrance, do still exist.

The GROTTO

Ordnance Survey reference SP 755667

The Grotto.

At the heart of Grotto Spinney is a mysterious Grotto built around a natural spring. Although the Grotto most probably dates from the 1770s, local folklore states that its construction could date from a much earlier period.

A series of traditions are associated with the Grotto, some in connection with Charles I, who was imprisoned at nearby Holdenby House in 1647, for he is known to have bowled at Boughton Hall at that time. He is said, for example, to have bathed there, using the Grotto as a dressing room. If these traditions really do refer to the Grotto rather than the ancient spring that rises there then the Grotto must pre-date the Wentworth period.

Although there have been traces found of early settlement activity in the fields adjacent to Grotto Spinney,[1] the Badeslade drawing of Boughton Hall which shows this part of the park in the background does not show the Grotto, despite showing more minor features such as Lord Vaux's Mount.

The ancient spring and the legends associated with it would have proved of such interest to William Wentworth that he probably either enhanced a ruinous primitive structure or built the Grotto structure afresh. He may even have elaborated on earlier stories and legends for the amusement of his circle of friends.

The Northamptonshire Mercury of 25 August 1810, reported that "at Boughton is a Spring, conceived to turn wood into stone. The truth is that it doth encrust anything with stone. I've seen a skull brought thence to Sydney College in Cambridge, candied over with stone...The skull was sent for by King Charles the First to satisfy his curiosity and again return to the college." Although the petrified skull loaned to Charles I does still survive in a carved wooden box dating from 1627, its origins are in Crete rather than Boughton! The skull is that of a child.[2]

Built from rough limestone blocks, the Grotto takes the form of a domed cave-like structure. Seemingly formed without the use of cement or mortar, the Grotto forms a perfect arch over the clear spring, known as "the Petrifying Spring", that rises there. The Grotto Spinney, in which the Grotto stands, is surrounded by the remains of a ha-ha wall, a device used on many occasions both at Boughton and at Wentworth Castle, the principal seat of the Wentworths.

In the Wentworths' time the Grotto spring would have been one of the water supplies for the artificial lake at the bottom of the valley. It would also have provided a picturesque watering hole for horses during a ride around the estate.

Mr Charles Kimbell wrote in 1946 that, around the turn of the century, "the spring cascaded into a gloomy pond whose waters were black through layers of decomposing leafage...About 50 years ago my father made a catch pit under the archway and piped the stream out of the little wood and down the valley. And so the petrified spring was incorporated in the village water system without apparently any ill effects on consumers."[3] Today, the spring rises crystal clear. The Grotto is now a Grade II listed structure.

The OBELISK

Ordnance Survey reference SP 753652

"We presently saw an obelisk before, belonging to the grounds of Lord Strafford, at Boughton", wrote an eighteenth-century traveller.[1] This impressive Obelisk was erected by William Wentworth in 1764 but is now surrounded by modern housing and its setting has been spoilt forever.

It was dedicated to the memory of William Cavendish, fourth Duke of Devonshire (1720–64) who, "when a young man, read with one of the incumbents of Boughton."[2] He was a man of considerable diplomatic subtlety, and was known for his incorruptibility. He was also perhaps one of the most reluctant and uncomfortable Prime Ministers in English history.

"A natural balance of judgement, prudence, patriotism, and above all a sense of service without self-seeking, were by common acclaim his characteristics. These qualities led Devonshire to appear briefly as Prime Minister from November 1756 until July 1757, to which he in no way aspired but undertook in the course of a crisis in time of war [the Seven Years War]."[3]

On his resignation he became Lord Chancellor until 1762, when the new King, George III, refused even to see him. Devonshire resigned immediately from all his offices and from political life, reminding us of Thomas Wentworth's problems on the accession of George I.

With his health rapidly declining, in the autumn of 1764 he went to the fashionable resort of Spa in the Ardennes, hoping the waters would cure him of dropsy. However, he suffered a stroke and died within a few days, prompting Horace Walpole to comment: "There's a chapter for moralizing! but five-and-forty, with forty thousand pounds a year, and happiness wherever he turned him! My reflection is, that it is a folly to be unhappy at anything, when felicity itself is such a phantom!"[4]

The Duke of Devonshire's fate obviously distressed William Wentworth

The Obelisk photographed c1910. The man standing alongside shows the scale of this structure.
(Courtesy: Northamptonshire Libraries)

as they had been acquainted since childhood; at the age of just 12, William wrote to his father: "We was last night at the Duke of Devonshire, it was a ball, thier was 8 couple...[including] Lord Heartington and...Mr Walpole."[5] Later he wrote from Boughton to William Cavendish that "my wishes for your happyness must extend, & the friendship and favor's you have always shown me exceeds what I could expect."[6] They even discussed the landscape design of their respective estates, with William Wentworth writing in 1756 that "We have hunted, rode & walk'd...& sketched out a much larger Park than I should have done without your opinion."[7]

The Obelisk, a Grade II listed structure, is the earliest such Egyptian-style monument in Northamptonshire and is constructed from a number of small stones. It originally bore the following inscription, including lines from Alexander Pope's *Essay on Man*, Epistle IV:

> This Obelisk was erected in the year 1764 in memory
> of His Grace William Cavendish Duke of Devonshire.
> There in the Rich
> The Honour'd Fam'd
> and Great,
> See the false scale
> Of Happiness
> Compleat! [8]

A past tenant of the farm on which this memorial stood before the housing estates were built had so much trouble from persons trespassing to read the inscription that it was erased by Peter Eaton Kimbell[9] on instructions from the Lord of the Manor.

In choosing an obelisk as a memorial, William Wentworth might have been inspired by Alexander Pope, a friend and neighbour of his father at Twickenham. Pope's mother, Edith (who was born only three miles from Wentworth Castle), died in the summer of 1733 and Pope commemorated her with an obelisk in his garden in 1735. Obelisks erected by the Wentworths at Wentworth Castle include Queen Anne's Obelisk, Lady Mary's Obelisk and the Birdwell Obelisk.

Mr Charles Kimbell wrote in 1944 that "The reason for the needle like pinnacle stone on the obelisk is due to the Government [?]; I believe, who had the stone fixed when I was a lad of 7 or 8. I remember well the flat appearance of the summit prior to repairs, also the erection of scaffolding round the obelisk and the stone being placed in position."[10] It should be noted that this was a "repair" probably due to the erosion of the original capping stone rather than an alteration to the Obelisk's original design, for obelisks are traditionally of this shape.

In 1929, long before the northwards expansion of Northampton and the building of the Obelisk Rise housing estate, it was reported that: "The obelisk stands on a raised mound of a circumference of about 55 yards, which is edged by rough stones to a depth of two feet. The site is the highest point in the district, and from it it is possible to see the line of the horizon all round. Thus the obelisk serves as a landmark, at a height of 450 feet above sea level, and is seen from a wide radius. The obelisk is built from blocks of white sandstone, from the old quarries at Kingsthorpe presumably. The stone seems to have been hardened by the weather, but where the surface has been broken and scratched away, the weather erosion has gone deep. The blocks are tongued together with bars of iron as well as mortared. So hard has this mortar become that in places where the stone has weathered badly it stands quite out on its own."[11]

This serious erosion led to a much more dangerous threat to the Obelisk in 1978 when a planning application was made to demolish the historic structure. The Milton Keynes Development Corporation even made an offer to take the monument down, stone by stone, to re-erect at the new town. However, after much deliberation, thankfully a decision was made to restore rather than demolish.

The SPECTACLE

Ordnance Survey reference SP 767660

To the eastern side of Boughton Park, standing beside Spectacle Lane, is a tall castellated arch dating from c1770, known as the Spectacle or Spectacles. It stands on the parish boundary between Boughton and Moulton, which was almost certainly the boundary for Boughton Park during the Wentworths' ownership.

This folly was designed as an eyecatcher, to be seen as a silhouette on the brow of a hill when viewed from the park. Local tradition says the Spectacle was positioned so that Moulton church would be framed by it when viewed from Boughton Park.

Drayton Arch photographed c1910.
(Courtesy: David Seccull)

The design for the Spectacle is almost identical to that of the Drayton Arch which dates from c1760 at Wroxton Abbey, near Banbury. Drayton Arch is reliably attributed to Sanderson Miller (1716–80),[1] who lived at Radway Grange in Warwickshire and was one of the leading exponents of the Gothic Revival in the eighteenth century. He was an adviser on landscape gardening at many estates in the Midlands, including Wroxton Abbey, the then seat of the North family, Earls of Guilford.

Although there is no record of Sanderson Miller having worked at

The Spectacle with its castellations intact, photographed c1915.
(Courtesy: Dave Martin)

Boughton, the two designs are so similar that William Wentworth must have at least used Miller's design as a basis for the Spectacle. Horace Walpole, who is recorded as being a visitor to Wroxton and an admirer of Miller's works there, may well have been the conveyor of ideas between the two estates, although geographical proximity may also explain the design replication. Indeed, one quotation from Horace Walpole seems to link the two arches together, when he says "Boughton and Drayton I have seen".[2]

The Spectacle comprises two slender semicircular towers with battlements, the rounded side facing Boughton Park. The towers are joined by an archway with battlements. Between the 1920s and 1950s some damage occurred to the wing walls, whilst c1950 the three crenellations above the keystone of the arch disappeared, possibly because of unfounded fears that their weight would collapse the arch. In reality, this action did more harm than good as it reduced the pressure on the arch, causing it to slip. Otherwise the Spectacle has survived intact for 225 years.

The reverse of the archway incorporates a dummy doorway beneath each tower. The only differences in design between the Spectacle and the Drayton Arch are that the former has wing walls, an open chimney in the reverse of each tower and smaller stones. One curious feature of the Spectacle is the existence of a small passage less than a foot in diameter through the southern tower. This must have been revealed when the archway was vandalised in the first half of this century. The passage, seemingly carved with a lime cement render, runs from the outside of the southern tower through to the limestone springer of the arch. Its purpose is a mystery, with no eighteenth-century building techniques known to require such a passage to run so deep into the structure.

After cracks had appeared in the archway of the Spectacle, a Grade II listed structure, it was rebuilt in 1992 by the Scott family, helped by small grants from Daventry District Council and Northamptonshire County Council.

NEW PARK BARN

Ordnance Survey reference SP 754669

New Park Barn photographed c1920.
(Courtesy: Northamptonshire Libraries)

Now converted into a private dwelling and renamed Fox Covert Hall, this structure has a style similar to the former Rockley Abbey, constructed by William Wentworth at Wentworth Castle. In 1760 Horace Walpole referred to William Wentworth "ornamenting a farm like the ruins of an abbey"[1] at his Yorkshire seat, when Wentworth constructed a farm in an ecclesiastical style even though it had never had any monastic connections.

Originally bearing a datestone of 1770 over the door, New Park Barn gives the appearance of a fortified castle with towers at either end and arrow-slit windows. In its original form the structure was castellated, although these features were removed c1929.

The sides facing Boughton feature large rusticated blocks of a soft white stone, possibly limestone. (This is the same material used to form the keystone and springers for the Spectacle.) The base of these walls and the whole of the rear are constructed with an inferior, yet more resilient, stone. Each turret at one stage had a single upper room, thatched above, with a door accessible only by ladder from the ground. The room at the southern end survives, but has been slated, possibly during the works of c1929.

Standing in a commanding position overlooking the valley, as with many of the follies associated with Boughton Park, this Grade II listed structure is designed only for viewing from the direction of the Hall. It is aligned so that the setting sun falls directly on to the structure when viewed from Boughton Hall. The Duke's Clump spinney to the west of New Park Barn features the remains of a ha-ha wall around its perimeter.

Fox Covert Hall today.

BUNKERS HILL FARM

Ordnance Survey reference SP 761666

Bunkers Hill from the south-west by George Clarke of Scaldwell (1790–1868).
(Courtesy: Northamptonshire Libraries)

Named in commemoration of the Battle of Bunkers Hill of 17 June 1775, the first major engagement of the American War of Independence. A Pyrrhic victory for Britain and a moral victory for the Americans, the battle came to symbolise the futility of British aggression and the moral righteousness of the American cause. Consequently, it was used to name features on estates whose owners were opposed to the war.

However, at Boughton the scenario is different. General Sir William Howe (1729–1814), who bravely led the British lines at the Battle of Bunkers Hill, was the nephew of William Wentworth, second Earl of Strafford.

Bunkers Hill from the south-west today.

View from the west showing the castellated gateway.

Very soon after the battle, on 10 October 1775, Howe became overall Commander-in-Chief of British forces in America, defeating the American colonists at Brandywine.

William Wentworth, therefore, erected what he described as "the house and offices built with battlements and arches"[1] in honour of the victory, rather than the folly of victory. It should be noted that Bunkers Hill Farm was by far the most functional of the structures in William Wentworth's Boughton folly landscape, perhaps reflecting the importance he attached to this British "victory".

Howe, by this stage, must have been quite fêted by his family: he was a friend of General Wolfe, leading a small group of two dozen hand-picked men to clear the path by which Wolfe scaled the Heights of Abraham to take Quebec in 1759; he had commanded a brigade at the siege of Belle Isle on the Brittany coast in 1761, and was Adjutant-General in the army at the conquest of Havana in 1762.

William Wentworth's views on the American War were in contrast to those of his friend Horace Walpole, who referred, in a letter of 1776 to William Wentworth, to the "subject on which I fear I am so unlucky as to differ very much with your Lordship, having always fundamentally disapproved our conduct with America."[2] In other correspondence dating from August 1775, Walpole refers to the British victory as "very equivocal...because the conquerors lost three to one more than the vanquished...we are a little disappointed indeed at their fighting at all."[3] A month later he was even more forthright, stating: "I am what I always was, a zealot for liberty in every part of the globe, and consequently...I most heartily wish success to the Americans."[4]

The two sides of Bunkers Hill Farm that face Boughton Park have elaborate castellated facades and quatrefoil windows – a design that extends even to the outbuildings. The datestone is inscribed "S 1776", the "S" standing for Strafford.

Like a number of the other follies in Boughton Park, Bunkers Hill (a Grade II listed structure) is positioned on the brow of a hill to achieve the greatest impact on the landscape.

The style of the structure conforms to the belief that "Few embellishments of an estate are more interesting than those small buildings which comprise the farm-offices and residences for the active, the superannuated, or other servants of the domain, particularly if they are designed in a manner conformable to the surrounding scenery, and distributed about the property with judgement. Such buildings, neat, clean, and in good repair, become testimonies of that liberality and care of his dependants that have always been distinguishing features in the character of a British gentleman."[5]

In a codicil to his will, dated 1786, William Wentworth left this farm with the parkland around it to his first footman, Samuel Redgrave.[6] Bunkers Hill and the land around it, from the stream at the bottom of the valley in the south to the Moulton/Pitsford road in the north and Spectacle Lane in the east, was rejoined to Boughton Park in 1863, when it was purchased by the Howard-Vyse family. At that stage there was no access between Bunkers Hill and the Moulton/Pitsford road, Bunkers Hill being linked to the outside world via what is now known as Butcher's Lane.

When the farm was sold in 1965, the property was still subject to the payment of £5 per year to the Earl of Strafford's Charity. This formed part of a "Grant of Annuity of £10 a Year to the Poor of Boughton and Pisford Dated 23rd November 1758...[to be distributed] on Christmas Day in every year for Ever...[for the] use and Benefit of the Poor of the Parishes of Boughton and Pisford."[7] The landholding responsible for the payment of the other £5 per annum, quite possibly located in Pitsford parish, is now unknown. Although the Earl of Strafford's Charity still exists, for the distribution of fuel to poor householders, the £5 annual payment by the owners of Bunkers Hill Farm was terminated in the mid 1980s by mutual consent as it had no worthwhile monetary value. However, it must be remembered that, in 1758, a sum of £10 was worth the equivalent of £604 today.[8]

Other landscape structures

Researches give tantalising clues regarding the existence of other structures within the Wentworths' Boughton landscape. Some, such as Lord Vaux's Mount and the Mount in the garden have already been mentioned. Unfortunately, few traces survive today of some of those features which further enhanced Boughton Park and its environs.

For example, Count Ferenc Széchényi, during his visit of 1787 noted: "There stands a kind of semi-circular temple made of laths covered with white linen, which can be rotated round an axle hidden in the ground, in accordance as one wishes to avoid the wind."[1]

It is not now possible to ascertain whether this is the same temple that appears on the 1794 map of Boughton Park.[2] This map clearly marks the position of "The Temple" (Ordnance Survey reference SP 749664) in the area now known as Little Brickhill Spinney, overlooking the western end of the lake on the Hall side of the valley. Although there are remnants of a circular section of ha-ha wall, any remaining physical evidence of the structure itself was destroyed when an internment camp was constructed on the site for Austrian and German prisoners of war during the First World War, and later used for displaced persons after the Second World War.

The lake at the base of the valley is a twentieth-century creation. However, its position is almost identical to a larger lake that existed during the Straffords' time, so clearly shown on Badeslade's 1732 drawing of Boughton Hall. A survey of 1792 refers to this as a fish pond of ten acres. By 1883, however, the original lakes had silted up.

When Bunkers Hill Farm was built by William Wentworth, the only access was via the track leading directly from Boughton Hall along the route of what is now known as Butcher's Lane. The small stone bridge (Ordnance

Survey reference SP 757664), built to cross what is in fact a tributary of the River Nene, formed the main artery of the park, linking the two sides of the valley. Its construction allowed William Wentworth to expand his landscape beyond the confines of the parkland adjacent to the Hall and into the surrounding countryside – a route used as a byway by local residents until the present day. A "Gothic Lodge" of 1770, mentioned by Dryden as being not far from Bunkers Hill, is probably New Park Barn.[3]

Although its origins are unknown, the Wentworths must have been charmed by the turf-cut maze located on their land at Boughton Green (centred on Ordnance Survey reference SP 764655). It is referred to variously as "Shepherds' Maze", "Shepherds' Race", "Shepherds' Ring", "Shepherds' Hay", "Shepherds' Run", "Cobblers' Round Maze" or "Church Maze". It was an intricate maze of circular form, 37 feet in diameter, ending in a definite spiral. By 1849 it is referred to as neglected, although later writers refer to its being in use, so it may have been recut in the mid nineteenth century. Although its shape was still determinable in the early years of this century, during the First World War trenches were inexplicably dug across it by soldiers in training and it was never restored.

Plan of the turf-cut maze formerly on Boughton Green.

Two theories as to its purpose or function have been espoused in the pages of Boughton's parish magazine. Firstly, "A great number of these mazes used to be in the neighbourhood of churches. They were probably used for penitential purposes or substitutes for pilgrimage. Folks who could not go to Jerusalem were allowed to compound, by walking round these mazes so many hundred or thousand times, repeating prayers. This was reckoned as a

Journey to Jerusalem."[4]

Secondly, it may have been "a pastime, which is enjoyed by the lower orders at the celebrated fair held in Boughton...A greenward circle of considerable size has been sunk about a foot below the surface of the Green as far back as memory can trace. A mazy path, rather more than a foot in width, is formed within by a trench, three or four inches wide, cut on each side of it; and the trial of skill consists in running the maze from the outside to the small circle in the centre in a given time, without crossing the boundaries of the path."[5]

Within the confines of Boughton Hall there still survive many examples of Gothic castellations dating from William Wentworth's time, found on an archway leading into the former kitchen garden, battlemented walls adjacent to the entrance connecting the Hall and the village, and on a pair of Grade II listed cottages within the park adjacent to the present cricket square.

The original castellated gateway connecting Boughton Hall to the village, photographed c1920.
(Courtesy: Northamptonshire Libraries)

The Church of St John the Baptist

Ordnance Survey reference SP 765656

Built alongside St John's Spring, an old pagan holy well, the Church of St John the Baptist is first mentioned in historical records in 1201. Although the date of its foundation is unknown, it has been suggested that its origins may be as early as the eighth century.[1]

The building consisted of a chancel, north chapel, nave, west tower and spire. The tower was of three stages with diagonal angle buttresses, pointed bell-chamber windows and a spire rising from behind battlemented parapets. There were three pointed two-light windows in the south wall. The nave and chancel had two large three-light east windows. Bridges, one of the earliest Northamptonshire historians, gave the length of the church and chancel as 69 feet 6 inches.[2] The wall and railings that now surround the churchyard are comparatively recent.

In an inventory of 1552, it is stated that of the church's two bells, one was broken down by thieves at night and sold to Goodman Frere at Ecton, whilst the other, featuring an impression of Henry III, is reputed to have gone to Moulton.

By 1719 the church lay in ruins, with no part of the roof remaining. This means that during the Wentworths' time at Boughton Hall they had, in effect, a true Gothic ruin on the edge of their park. This may explain why, despite all their building on the estate and the moral obligation of the Lord of the Manor to maintain the fabric of the church, there is no evidence of their attempting any restoration work.

The Rectors of Boughton[3] during the Wentworths' ownership of Boughton were: Charles Briscoe (c1674–1748, Rector 1700–48), the son of Sir John Briscoe, whose mortgage of the estate was foreclosed by Lord Ashburnham five years before the sale of the Boughton estate to Thomas

Engraving showing Boughton Church c1760.

Wentworth; William Jackson (c1716–95, Rector 1748–69), who was later to become Rector of Pitsford; William Rowley (1722–75, Rector 1769–75), and John Dixon (1746–1816, Rector 1776–1816), who was also appointed Rector of Toddington in 1788, presumably so that William Wentworth could be sure of a proper interment, by a Rector known to him, into the Wentworth family vault in that village. In a codicil to his will in 1789, William Wentworth specifically requests: "I would be buryed as privately at Toddington as possible."[4]

The last record of a wedding at the old Boughton church, according to the registers, was in 1708, with the steeple and tower falling c1785. In the early nineteenth century, stone was taken from the ruin to enlarge the chapel, now the church, in the village.

In 1930 it was reported that "some thoughtless and ill-disposed persons have been guilty of acts of desecration"[5] which further damaged the structure before, in 1931, "The East End Wall of the old Church has been successfully buttressed to prevent further collapse."[6] Today the ruin is an evocative if somewhat neglected sight, with ivy covering most of the remaining walls.

The church and graveyard stand on sloping ground at the edge of a roughly triangular plot of land known as Boughton Green (centred on Ordnance Survey reference SP 764655) – the site of an ancient fair lasting three days on the vigil, day and morrow of St John the Baptist. Granted a Royal Charter by Edward III on 28 February 1351, it flourished as one of the country's leading fairs for many years. It is recorded in the *Northamptonshire Mercury* that, in 1720, Thomas Wentworth intended to be "down at his Seat at Boughton during the Fair."[7] A year later, Thomas Wentworth is said to be "pleased to give a Hat, value One Guinea, to be played for...at Cudgels."[8] However, despite the patronage of the Wentworths, on whose land the fair was held, by the end of the nineteenth century the fair's importance had declined.

Boughton Church today with St John's Spring in the foreground.

Perhaps the best account of the fair in the eighteenth century is by Wentworth himself, when he wrote that the "Fair has from the Time of King John [reigned 1199–1216] been look'd upon as a great advantage to the...poorer sort of People of those parts, who furnish themselves, once a year with all sort of Husbandry Tools & utensels at cheaper rates than they can in ye Markets & those that make those sort of things are but poor & sell them for little profit.

"This Fair is kept in an open field, halfe a mile from ye village of Boughton, and Booths...are Erected by ye Lord of ye Mannor for that time only...and besides other advantages that ye Tenants on the Estate receive from ye Conveniency of the Fair, ye Village of Boughton have a right during ye Time of that Fair to sell ale in evry House, which turns greatly to their profit.

"This Fair is in most respects Different from others. It is the sole property of one man [the Lord of the Manor] which no other Fair in that neighbourhood is."[9]

In the 1880s it was recorded that "The last and greatest day [of the fair] was crowded with many incidents, for the cattle fair held on June 25 was understood to be one of the largest of its kind in the country; buyers and sellers came from far away regions to attend it...As night approached the crowds increased. Drunken men staggered everywhere. Fighting became contagious."[10] Eventually "Owing to the complaints of the local inhabitants the Fair was closed by Sir Richard Granville Howard-Vyse in 1916. On June 16th of that year an Order was received from the Home Secretary putting an end to the Charter."[11] In 1942 the green was ploughed up, perhaps for the first time in its history, to assist with the "war effort".

HOLLY LODGE

Ordnance Survey reference SP 769658

Holly Lodge – inspired by the Wentworths' Gothic style.

Holly Lodge was designed by the Northampton-based architect Alexander Milne for Philadelphus Jeyes. It stands beside the boundary of the former Wentworth estate. This imposing castellated residence was built between 1857 and 1861 in a style very sympathetic to the traditions of the eighteenth-century structures elsewhere in Boughton Park. The original architect's drawings for Holly Lodge clearly show that a smaller existing structure was incorporated within the design.[1] Traces of this can still be seen on the eastern wall of the property.

Also incorporated within the design, on the Moulton/Boughton road frontage, is an almost exact replica of the Spectacle which stands only 250 yards away from Holly Lodge. Originally there were, in fact, only differences of detail between the two. The walls to either side of the Holly Lodge arch feature stone panels with carved cherubs.

Philadelphus Jeyes opened a "chymist" shop in the Drapery, Northampton, in 1810. Although the shop survives it is now in different hands. Philadelphus's younger brother, John, founded Jeyes Sanitary Compounds – famous throughout the world for Jeyes Fluid, one of 21 patents held by John Jeyes.

The Farm Implement Gates at the entrance to Holly Lodge were designed by Philadelphus Jeyes and may be unique. The manufacturers were Allchin of Northampton, later famous for their traction engines. The gates include replicas of two hay forks, two sickles, a scythe, a rake, a shepherd's crook, a ditch cutter, a stable fork, a flail, a spade and a woodman's axe. They were erected in 1861.

Holly Lodge, a Grade II listed structure, remains in the Jeyes family to this day.

The famous Farm Implement Gates at Holly Lodge.

The problem today

Having survived almost intact for more than 200 years, Boughton Park now faces two very real threats: firstly, from quarrying, as there are mineral extraction rights on the northern side of the valley; secondly, from a proposed bypass.

Northamptonshire County Council proposes to construct a bypass road linking the Moulton Park Industrial Estate and the A45 west of Northampton, near Harpole. The proposed route of the bypass – through the centre of Boughton Park – has been agreed at a full meeting of the Northamptonshire County Council, although planning permission for the section relating to Boughton Park has not, as yet, been put forward for approval.

This County Council decision came despite dissent from Daventry District Council, Moulton Parish Council and the Country Landowners Association. Subsequently, recognised national bodies such as English Heritage, the Garden History Society, the Folly Fellowship, the Georgian Group, ICOMOS UK and the Temple Trust have raised strong objections to this potential destruction of an exemplary part of Northamptonshire's heritage.

Two options were originally considered – Option 1, the shortest route which would travel closest to Northampton and, Option 2, which cuts through open countryside, including the unique eighteenth-century landscape of Boughton Park.

If the Option 2 route were to be built as currently planned, then New Park Barn, the Grotto, Bunkers Hill Farm, the Spectacle and Holly Lodge would be separated from Boughton Hall, the Hawking Tower and the Church of St John the Baptist. This would ruin the integrity of this historic landscape whilst also risking actual damage to the structures themselves – in particular the Grotto, the Spectacle and Holly Lodge, due to their close proximity to the proposed route.

English Heritage have listed Boughton Park on their *Register of Parks and Gardens of Special Historic Interest in England* to increase awareness of the existence of the park and to encourage its protection and conservation. This responsibility now rests with the Northamptonshire County Council.

Will this nationally important historic landscape be protected for future generations? More than 50 years ago, Charles E Kimbell wrote: "Unfortunately the army of planners, who live mainly at a distance and to whom Boughton is only a name, have ignored, so far, the united opposition of its residents to some of their plans...Picturesque old Boughton does not deserve such a melancholy fate."[1]

Let us hope that in today's enlightened, conservationist world we do not see history repeating itself...

Notes

Abbreviations
NRO = Northampton Record Office.
SP = Strafford Papers, British Library Manuscript Collection.

The Earls of Strafford
1. Strafford is the name of the Wapentake (division of a shire) in which Wentworth Woodhouse is situated. Geoffrey H White (editor), *GEC Complete Peerage*, 1953 edition, vol 12/I p326 note a.
2. Anne Johnson was daughter of Sir Henry Johnson of Bradenham, Buckinghamshire and Toddington, Bedfordshire. *ibid.*, pp330–331.
3. Mount Lebanon, on the banks of the River Thames.
4. Wentworth Castle, his principal seat, at Stainborough, Yorkshire.
5. NRO, Howard-Vyse Collection, box 7, parcel 3, dated 6 October 1739.
6. This is documented in great detail by Michael Charlesworth, Patrick Eyres, Wendy Frith, "The Wentworths", *New Arcadian Journal*, No31/32, Summer/Autumn 1991.
7. Geoffrey H White, *op.cit.*, p331 note d.
8. Howard Colvin, *Biographical Dictionary of British Architects 1600–1840*, 1978, p879.
9. Geoffrey H White, *op.cit.*, p332 note a.
10. Horace Walpole, *The History of the Modern Taste in Gardening*, 1995, p58. (Based on the 1782 edition.)

Horace Walpole and other influences
1. Derek Jarrett, *Britain 1688–1815*, 1965, p370. In reality the rebuilding and extending of Strawberry Hill took from 1748 to 1792 (*Country Life*, 7 June 1973).
2. Wilmarth S Lewis (editor), *The Yale Edition of Horace Walpole's Correspondence*, 1973, vol 35, p332, letter dated 3 July 1769.
3. James J Cartwright (editor), *The Wentworth Papers 1705–1739*, 1883, p462, letter dated December 1730.
4. From a copy of William Wentworth's will dated 20 October 1774 deposited at Northampton Library, Local History Section, Broadsheet Collection.
5. Information provided by Mrs Sam Davies of the Bank of England in a letter to the author dated 3 November 1994.
6. Wilmarth S Lewis, *op.cit.*, vol 35, introduction pXI.
7. Paget Toynbee (editor) "Horace Walpole's Journal of his Visits to Country Houses etc." *The Walpole Society*, vol XVI, 1928, p28.
8. Horace Walpole, *op.cit.*, p60.
9. Paget Toynbee (editor), *Letters of Horace Walpole*, 1903, vol III, p442, letter from Horace Walpole to Richard Bentley, August 1756.
10. Paget Toynbee, "Horace Walpole's Journal of his Visits to Country House etc", *op.cit.*, p65.
11. Quoted from a letter to the author dated 18 October 1994.
12. James J Cartwright, *op.cit.*, p443, letter dated 31 August 1717.
13. British Library Manuscript Collection, ref 22221, f140.
14. *ibid.*, f417.
15. James J Cartwright, *op.cit.*, p454, letter dated 20 July 1725.
16. *ibid.*, p455, letter dated 5 August 1725.
17. Wilmarth S Lewis, *op.cit.*, vol 35, p148, letter from Horace Walpole to Richard Bentley dated September 1753.
18. Morris R Brownell, *Alexander Pope and the Arts of Georgian England*, 1978, p183.

Boughton Hall
1. The early history of Boughton Hall is chronicled in detail by Susan Ranson, *Boughton Hall*, 1969.
2. James J Cartwright, *op.cit.*, p332, letter dated 8 May 1713.
3. *ibid.*, p443, letter dated 31 August 1717.
4. SP, ref 22251, dated February–May 1719.
5. *ibid.*, dated 1719.
6. *ibid.*
7. James J Cartwright, *op.cit.*, p447, letter dated 10 December 1719.
8. *Boughton Parish Magazine*, April 1944.
9. John Bridges, *History and Antiquities of the County of Northamptonshire*, 1791, p411.

10. NRO, ref ZA 8011K. Anon, but dating from between 1764 (the building of the Obelisk to which this document refers) and 1791 (William Wentworth's death). These pages, pp549–560, are headed "Tour thro' the Midland Counties etc" but unfortunately are separated from the volume into which they were originally bound. This work cannot be traced in the British Library.
11. George Baker, *History and Antiquities of the County of Northampton*, 1822–30, vol I, p35
12. *Boughton Parish Magazine, op.cit.*

Boughton Park
1. Quoted from a letter to the author dated 18 June 1994.
2. James J Cartwright, *op.cit.*, p443, letter dated 31 August 1717.
3. SP, *op.cit.*, letter from John Rose dated 24 October 1717.
4. *ibid.*, dated 16 February 1718.
5. *ibid.*, dated 9 February 1718.
6. HMSO, *An Inventory of the Historical Monuments in the County of Northamptonshire*, 1981, vol III, p14.
7. James J Cartwright, *op.cit.*
8. SP, *op.cit.*, letter from Edward Briggs dated 11 November 1721.
9. *ibid.*, dated 26 November 1721.
10. *ibid.*, dated 11 December 1721.
11. *ibid.*, dated 28 January 1721.
12. *ibid.*, dated 17 December(?) 1722.
13. *ibid.*, dated (?) February 1722.
14. *ibid.*, letter from Thomas Badeslade dated 16 January 1732.
15. *ibid.*, undated.
16. *ibid.*, dated 30 May 1732.
17. *ibid.*, letter from John Worley dated 23 June 1737.
18. *ibid.*, dated 7 June 1737.
19. József Sisa, "Count Ferenc Széchényi's visit to English Parks and Gardens in 1787", *Garden History*, vol 22, Summer 1994, pp64–66.
20. NRO, ref ZA 8011K, *op.cit.*
21. Arthur Young, *A Farmer's Tour through the East of England*, 1771, pp44–45.
22. NRO, Howard-Vyse Collection ref 5313, *Plan of the Lands & Premises allotted to Richard William Howard-Vyse*, 1794.
23. George Baker, *op.cit.*, p31.
24. Susan Ranson, *op.cit.*, p24.
25. Public Record Office, Kew, ref OS5/19: *The County of Northamptonshire Surveyed and Planned by the late Mr Thomas Eyre of Kettering, revised by the late Mr Thomas Jefferys Geographer to the King and engraved by William Faden 1779. Second Edition revised and corrected 1791*.
26. Northampton Library Local History Section, Broadsheet Collection, from a codicil to William Wentworth's will dated 8 August 1782.
27. Charles E Kimbell, *Boughton in the '80s*, c1940, p5.
28. Quoted from English Heritage's register entry for Boughton Park, 20 June 1995.
29. L B Seeley (editor), *Horace Walpole and his World*, 1892, fourth edition, pp115–116. Note that "Vauxhall" refers to Vauxhall Gardens in London, a fashionable place of entertainment during the late eighteenth century.

The Hawking Tower
1. Information provided by Keith Adams in a letter to the author dated 23 October 1994.
2. Information provided by Mrs Mary Rowden.
3. Information provided by Mr Esmond Kimbell.
4. David Hey, *Wentworth Castle*, 1991, p11.
5. Wilmarth S Lewis, *op.cit.*, vol 35, p279, letter dated 28 August 1756.

The Grotto
1. Found by local archaeologist, Mr Richard Hollowell. Information provided by Mr Esmond Kimbell.
2. Information provided by Nicholas Rogers of Sidney Sussex College, Cambridge in a letter to the author dated 17 March 1995.
3. *Boughton Parish Magazine*, February 1946.

The Obelisk
1. NRO, ZA 8011K *op.cit.*
2. L F Salzman (editor), "A History of Northamptonshire", *The Victoria History of the Counties of England*,

1937, vol IV p77 note 1.
3. Peter Brown and Karl Schweizer, *The Devonshire Diary 1759–62*, 1982, p1.
4. John Pearson, *Stags & Serpents*, 1983, p85.
5. James J Cartwright, *op.cit.*, p479, letter dated 29 March 1733.
6. Devonshire Papers, 413–0, dated 25 May 1755.
7. *ibid.*, 413–8, dated 28 December 1756. Unfortunately, it is not recorded whether this comment relates to Boughton Park or Wentworth Castle.
8. Christopher A Markham, *The Stone Crosses of the County of Northampton*, 1901, pp22–23.
9. *Boughton Parish Magazine*, May 1928: "Mr P E Kimbell...For many years connected with the Estate in an official capacity."
10. *ibid.*, June 1944.
11. *ibid.*, May 1944, quoting from the *Northampton County Magazine*, March 1929, p84.

The Spectacle
1. Information supplied by Mr William Hawkes. For more details refer to: William Hawkes, "Miller's Work at Wroxton" *Cake & Cockhorse*, Winter 1969, pp98–110.
2. NRO, *Northamptonshire Past & Present*, 1966–67, vol IV, p50, letter dated 10 October 1780.

New Park Barn
1. Paget Toynbee, *op.cit.*, p28.

Bunkers Hill Farm
1. From a codicil to William Wentworth's will, dated 11 January 1786, at Northampton Library, Local History Section, Broadsheet Collection.
2. Wilmarth S Lewis, *op.cit.*, vol 35, p352, letter dated 2 November 1776.
3. *ibid.*, vol 24, pp119–120, letter dated 3 August 1775 to Sir Horace Mann.
4. L B Seeley, *op.cit.*, p152, letter dated 7 September 1775 to Sir Horace Mann.
5. John B Papworth, *Rural Residences*, 1818, p21.
6. See note 1 above.
7. NRO, 39p/23.
8. Information supplied by Mrs Sam Davies of the Bank of England in a letter to the author dated 3 November 1994.

Other landscape structures
1. József Sisa, *op.cit.*, p66.
2. NRO, Howard-Vyse Collection, ref 5313, *op.cit.*
3. Nikolaus Pevsner, *Northamptonshire*, second edition 1973, p110.
4. *Boughton Parish Magazine*, June 1925.
5. *ibid.*, May 1945.

The Church of St John the Baptist
1. Information from Stephen Trott, Rector of Boughton.
2. John Bridges, *op.cit.*, pp410–413.
3. Rev H I Longden, *Northamptonshire and Rutland Clergy from 1500*, 1938–43, Briscoe vol 2 p229, Jackson vol 7 p249, Rowley vol 11 p271, Dixon vol 4 p101.
4. From a codicil to William Wentworth's will dated 24 April 1789, at Northampton Library Local History Section, Broadsheet Collection.
5. *Boughton Parish Magazine*, May 1930.
6. *ibid.*, October 1931.
7. *Northamptonshire Mercury*, 20 June 1720.
8. *ibid.*, 5 June 1721.
9. SP, Add 63474, f113.
10. Charles E Kimbell, *op.cit.*, pp31–33.
11. *Boughton Parish Magazine*, August 1943.

Holly Lodge
1. Shown to the author by Mr Anthony Jeyes.

The problem today
1. Charles E Kimbell, *op.cit.*, pp51–52.